User Surveys in College Libraries

CLIP]   DATE DUE

Compiled by

Doreen Kopycinski
Catalog Librarian
Lehigh University
Bethlehem, Pennsylvania

Kimberley Sando
Systems Librarian
DeSales University
Center Valley, Pennsylvania

College Library Information Packet Committee
College Libraries Section
Association of College and Research Libraries
A Division of the American Library Association

The paper used in this publication meets the minimum requirements of the American National Standard for Information Sciences-Permanence of Paper for Printed Library Materials, ANSI Z39.48-1992.

Library of Congress Cataloging-in-Publication Data

User surveys in college libraries / compiled by Doreen Kopycinski, Kimberley Sando.
     p. cm. -- (CLIP note ; #38)
 Includes bibliographical references and index.
 ISBN-13: 978-0-8389-8433-8 (pbk. : alk. paper)
 1. Academic libraries--United States--Use studies. I. Kopycinski, Doreen. II. Sando, Kimberley. III. Association of College and Research Libraries. College Library Information Packet Committee.
 Z675.U5U86 2007
 025.5'8770973--dc22
                          2007016831

Copyright © 2007 by the American Library Association. Portions of this publication may be photocopied for the noncommercial purpose of scientific or educational advancement granted by Sections 107 and 108 of the Copyright Revision Act of 1976.

Printed on recycled paper.

Printed in the United States of America.

12 11 10 09 08 07   5 4 3 2 1

Cover design by Jim Lange Design

TABLE OF CONTENTS

Porter Henderson Library
Angelo State University
San Angelo, Texas

Stanley Library
Ferrum College
Ferrum, Virginia

James B. Duke Library
Furman University
Greenville, South Carolina

Raugust Library
Jamestown College
Jamestown, North Dakota

Jackson Library
Lander University
Greenwood, South Carolina

J. Spencer & Patricia Standish Library
Siena College
Loudonville, New York

Lavery Library
St. John Fisher College
Rochester, New York

Tisch Library
Tufts University
Medford, Massachusetts

Schmidt Library
York College of Pennsylvania
York, Pennsylvania

Porter Henderson Library
Angelo State University
San Angelo, Texas

Weis Library
Columbia Union College
Takoma Park, Maryland

Raugust Library
Jamestown College
Jamestown, North Dakota

Simpson Library
Mary Washington College
Fredericksburg, Virginia

O'Grady Library
Saint Martins University
Lacey, Washington

Miller F. Whittaker Library
South Carolina State University
Orangeburg, South Carolina

Lavery Library
St. John Fisher College
Rochester, New York

Schmidt Library
York College of Pennsylvania
York, Pennsylvania

Ross Pendergraft Library
Arkansas Tech University
Russellville, Arkansas

Golden Library
Eastern New Mexico University
Portales, New Mexico

Carol Grotnes Belk Library
Elon University
Elon, North Carolina

James Earl Carter Library
Georgia Southwestern State University
Americus, Georgia

Duggan Library
Hanover College
Hanover, Indiana

Schewe Library
Illinois College
Jacksonville, Illinois

Dick Smith Library
Tarleton State University
Stephenville, Texas

Carol Grotnes Belk Library
Elon University
Elon, North Carolina

Dick Smith Library
Tarleton State University
Stephenville, Texas

CLIP Notes Committee

Ann M. Watson (Chair)
Denison University Libraries
Granville, OH

Amy J. Arnold
East Tennessee State University
Johnson City, TN

Doreen M. Kopycinski
Lehigh University
Bethlehem, PA

Rachel C. Crowley
Briar Cliff University
Sioux City, IA

Cherie Alexandra Madarash-Hill
University of Central Arkansas
Conway, AR

Nancy E. Frazier
Buffalo State College
Buffalo, NY

Debbie L. Malone
DeSales University
Center Valley, PA

Gillian S. Gremmels
Wartburg College
Waverly, IA

Myrna Joy McCallister
Indiana State University
Terre Haute, IN

Ms. Elizabeth A. Kocevar-Weidinger
Longwood University
Farmville, VA

Leslie L. Morgan
University of Notre Dame
Notre Dame, IN

Acknowledgements

Many thanks to our editor, Deb Malone. Feedback to feed the
revision process is so important and necessary--Deb gave us a lot of
much appreciated food for thought.

I'm forever thankful for my husband, Dave, for his constant patience,
support and love. He's the gift that keeps on giving. *DK*

Thank you to my entire family for their love and support, and to Deb
for her guidance and patience. *KS*

INTRODUCTION

INTRODUCTION

*Objective*_____

In 1980, ACRL's Continuing Education Committee of the College Libraries Section published the first CLIP (College Library Information Packet) Note, *Performance Appraisal*. Since then, the CLIP Notes Committee has been facilitating the publication of various CLIP Notes to provide practical support and ideas to college libraries as they pursue development of policies, practices, and procedures essential to their operations.

The first edition of the CLIP Note *User Surveys in College Libraries* in 1995 proved to be a popular publication, as libraries strive to improve their services to their user communities by attempting to discover their needs and expectations. In the past ten years, the use of surveys in libraries has evolved with the development of online tools and services, so it was deemed appropriate to provide a second edition of this publication.

*Background*_____

In 2005, the American Institute of Public Opinion, the organization that administers the Gallup Poll, celebrated its 70th anniversary. In his book *Survey Research Methods*, Earl Babbie notes that social surveys began their development as a tool in the late 19th century, using one interesting example of a political, attitudinal survey that was conducted by Karl Marx who surveyed "French workers to determine the extent of exploitation by employers...while 25,000 questionnaires were mailed out, there is no record of any being returned,"[1] a response rate many of us fear!

Survey research grew and was refined throughout the 20th century and, within the past ten years, survey methods have shifted from paper, telephone, and focus groups to online surveys. However, the recent past has also seen a less then positive development in survey research, that of a decline in response rates. Martha Kropf and Johnny Blair cite one example in which "the average number of call attempts that the Survey Research Center at the University of Maryland had to make to complete an interview increased almost 30% over the 10 years

---

1. Babbie, *Survey Research Methods*, 42.

from 1989 to 1998."[2] Surveyors are utilizing incentives to help increase response rates and have found that incentives have a positive impact.

Survey Procedure

Using the CLIP Notes guidelines, the compilers developed a survey based on that found in the 1995 *User Surveys in College Libraries* to allow for an historical comparison. A first draft of the survey was tested on a sample group, and the survey was edited based on feedback. The compilers used the online tool SurveyMonkey.com to manage the survey and, in May 2006, invited librarians representing 251 libraries to respond (the respondent list is compiled by the CLIP Notes Committee of those who are interested in participating in CLIP Notes surveys); 133 responded, for a response rate of 53%.

Although this is considered an adequate response rate,[3] the compilers were curious to see if the respondents' survey use was representative of the sample as a whole. The compilers sent a follow-up to those who had not responded, requesting response to one question from the survey: "Has your library conducted at least one survey, within the past five years that included questions about library use?" The expectation was that those who did not respond had not conducted surveys and decided their responses were not necessary. Although the response rate of this second survey was low (there were only 39 of 118 responses, or 33%), it is interesting to note that 85% said they had conducted surveys and 15% had not, which is comparable to the outcome of the initial survey (for which 87% said they had and 13% had not).

Notes on Survey Statistics

It is important to note that, in the previous edition of this title, some survey questions limited respondents to "check one only." Before performing the survey for this edition, a test run of the survey was held. Test respondents requested that the "check one only" response be reworded to "check all that apply" to allow for those instances when an institution administered more than one survey in the past five years, especially since one survey might have differed from another, warranting multiple responses for multiple surveys. By changing this

---

2. Kropf and Blair, "Eliciting Survey Cooperation," 559.
3. Babbie, *The Practice of Social Research*, 261.

wording, there are instances when one respondent might have multiple responses to a question (since they could "check all that apply") whereas, in the first survey, only one response was allowed. The reader should take this into consideration when comparisons of this survey's results are provided with the previous edition, as is seen throughout the *Analysis of Survey Results*, found on pages 13-17 of this book.

ANALYSIS OF SURVEY RESULTS

1. Institutional Profile (Questions #1-9)

Respondents provided basic contact information, and institutional information regarding the size of the student body and the size of the library's staff. The final question in this section served as a breaking off point for those whose libraries had administered user surveys in the past five years (who were then directed to complete questions #10-28) and those who had not (directed to complete questions #29-30).

2. Survey Information: Background (Questions #10-21)

To gauge the motivation for, development of, and practical aspects of user surveys, respondents were asked basic questions about the use of surveys in their institution.

Type of survey and method (Questions #10-12)

As might be expected, there has been a revolution in survey methodology. Ten years ago, 90% of respondents noted reliance on a paper survey. That has dropped to 31%, with the majority of responses (48%) noting use of computer-based surveys. In 2001, the inaugural issue of the journal *portal: Libraries and the Academy* included an article describing the development of LibQUAL+™, an online survey instrument, and, since then, many libraries have made use of this library-specific tool (36 of our respondents have done so). Other online survey tools include MISO, the Merged Information Services Organizations survey instrument (developed by Bryn Mawr College, Bates College, Middlebury College, the University of Richmond, and Wellesley College) and SurveyMonkey.com (which facilitates the online management of an institutions locally-developed survey instrument).

Do you offer an incentive (award, name placed in drawing, etc.) for completion of the survey(s)? (Question #13)

Over half of our respondents (54%) offer an incentive for survey participation. Recent literature has lamented the drop in participation in user surveys, tying it to factors such as the ubiquity of both telemarketers and the call blocking function of telephones, decreasing voter turnout, and lower civic engagement.[4] Other studies note increases in response rates achieved with the use of incentives.[5] Our respondents reported a variety of incentives, a list of which can be perused in the results on page 29.

Survey writing, distribution, and compilation. (Questions #16-19)

A greater variety of responses to the question "The survey was written by..." (question #16) were seen for this survey than the first one administered ten years ago. In 1995, 52% of responses noted that one staff member, either alone or with support from others, was responsible for writing the survey. For this second edition, that figure has dropped to 34%. Respondents in 2006 relied largely on sources outside the library's staff, with 37% noting that they had consulted with non-librarians, compared with 20% ten years ago. Some of those sources were close to home (such as institutional support, campus library committee, students from a social research class) but it was primarily organizations off campus (e.g. LibQUAL+™, MISO) that assisted our respondents.

Accompanying declines are seen for the additional questions regarding distribution and compilation. For both, there was more than a 10% decline in management by one staff member, whether alone or with additional staff support. As can be gleaned from casual comparison and confirmed with this survey, compared with ten years ago, more institutions are using outside sources to develop and manage their user surveys.

Use of sources for the development of the survey (Questions #20-21)

Despite the proliferation of literature on the topic, there was a 10% increase in those who did not use any resources in the development of their survey. At the same time, there was an overall decrease of 28.7% in reported use of any literature sources. One possible explanation is lack of necessity, again affected by the movement towards outsourcing.

---

4. Kropf and Blair, "Eliciting Survey Cooperation," 559-560.
5. Kropf and Blair, "Eliciting Survey Cooperation;" Sax, Gilmartin, and Bryant, "Assessing Response Rates;" Szelenyi, Bryant, and Lindholm, "What Money Can Buy."

3. Survey Information: Use and Evaluation (Questions #22-27)

Along with incentives, users will be more likely to complete surveys if they see that the previous survey afforded change. Talbot, Lowell, and Martin state, "users are intimately involved in the process and their feedback needed not only to be taken seriously, but also acted upon."[6] This idea is also reflected later in the survey in comments given to advise those considering doing a survey. Libraries need to communicate if nothing else the results of the survey. Almost all of the respondents (99.8%) reported taking some kind of action with the survey results, such as 11.7% made actual changes in policies and procedures. Of the 412 responses, 72 (17.5%) noted changes in services or staffing.

As Hiller notes: "Rapid changes in library services and operations, demands for internal institutional accountability, and assessment expectations by external accrediting agencies have contributed to further development and application of user surveys with academic libraries during the past decade."[7] This helps to explain the large number of respondents (81%) who sought out expertise on campus for assistance with formulating and implementing the surveys. In the first edition, a mere 16% found the need to seek out expert advice and assistance. Users are savvier. With the prevalence of online survey tools, the vast amount of information librarians are seeking to gain through a survey, and the time, and sometimes money, it requires to create surveys, it is almost a necessity to seek help to assure the process is smooth and worthwhile.

Did the results of the survey provide you with useful information (Question #23) and *How satisfied were you with the process you used? (Question #25)*

In the first edition, 84% found the information provided from the surveys to be "useful" or "very useful" and 86% were "satisfied" or "very satisfied" with the process. The numbers for this second edition are almost identical: 86.4% of responses found the information received to be useful and the same percentage were satisfied with the process that was used. The percentage of respondents who were "dissatisfied" with the process used went down from 6% to 2.7% and only .9% found the information received from the survey "not very useful," down from 2%. No significant changes are noted in this area of the survey.

---

6. Talbot, Lowell, and Martin, "From the User's Perspective," 358.
7. Hiller, "Assessing User Needs," 606.

Check all problems that occurred (Question #26)

Problems with surveys are the same today as they were ten years ago, including low response rates and the challenges of reaching both users and non-users. An interesting approach found in the literature with which to target users is the use of a pop-up survey question on library webpages or online catalogs. These point-of-use surveys provide year round assessment of services. Another suggestion made by Plosker in "Conducting User Surveys: An Ongoing Information Imperative" is to "segment your users . . . [or] 'cataloging' your patrons into groups that share similar perspectives and motivation for using information."[8] He suggests that survey information that is more focused becomes more effective; this is also suggested in the responses to question #27 "What advice would you give to another librarian planning a survey?" Librarians surveyed suggest that keeping surveys short and focused on one issue would be the ideal scenario.

What advice would you give to another librarian planning a survey? (Question #27)

Advice for librarians planning a survey remained similar to what appeared in the first edition, such as planning and keeping the survey short and focused. These views are also reflected in the recent literature. Testing both the survey questions and the survey instrument were also deemed important; testing the survey instrument was not noted as a concern ten years ago.

4. **Survey Information: No Surveys Within the Past Five Years (Questions #29-30)**

For those who answered the question dealing with the library's status on surveys (question #9), 87% have conducted surveys within the past five years. The number one reason that prevented the remaining 13% from conducting a survey was lack of staff time (40%). Staff time is a problem that is often unlikely to be resolved, but it does appear to be getting better as, ten years ago, 74% of respondents stated lack of staff time as an issue. Another issue was skepticism about the benefits of surveys (10%), a decrease from the 20% previously reported.

---

8. Plosker, "Conducting User Surveys," 65.

BIBLIOGRAPHY

BIBLIOGRAPHY

Babbie, Earl R. *Survey Research Methods*. Belmont, Calif.: Wadsworth Publishing, 1973.

_____. *The Practice of Social Research.* 10th ed. Belmont, Calif.: Thomson Wadsworth, 2004.

Bradburn, Norman, Seymour Sudman, and Brian Wansink. *Asking Questions: The Definitive Guide to Questionnaire—For Market Research, Political Polls, and Social and Health Questionnaires*. Rev ed. San Francisco: Jossey-Bass, 2004.

Cook, Colleen, Fred Heath, Bruce Thompson, and Russel Thompson. "The Search for New Measures: The ARL LibQUAL+Project—A Preliminary Report." *portal: Libraries and the Academy* 1, no. 1 (2001):103-112.

Fowler, Floyd J., Jr. *Survey Research Methods.* 3rd ed. Thousand Oaks, Calif.: Sage Publications, 2002.

Hiller, Steve. "Assessing User Needs, Satisfaction, and Library Performance at the University of Washington Libraries." *Library Trends* 49, no. 4 (2001):605-625.

Kidston, James S. "The Validity of Questionnaire Responses." *Library Quarterly* 55, no. 2 (1985):133-150.

Kropf, Martha E., and Johnny Blair. "Eliciting Survey Cooperation: Incentives, Self-interest, and Norms of Cooperation." *Evaluation Review* 29, no. 6 (2005):559-575.

Kyrillidou, Martha, and Fred M. Heath. *Measuring Service Quality*. Champaign, Ill.: Univ. of Illinois Graduate School of Library and Information Science, 2001.

Lancaster, F. W. *If You Want to Evaluate Your Library. . .* 2nd ed. Champaign, Ill.: Univ. of Illinois, Graduate School of Library and Information Science, 1993.

Morgan, David L., ed. *Successful Focus Groups: Advancing the State of the Art*. Newbury Park, Calif.: Sage Publications, 1993.

Payne, Stanley L. *The Art of Asking Questions*. Princeton, N.J.: Princeton Univ. Press, 1979.

Plosker, George R. "Conducting User Surveys: An Ongoing Information Imperative." *Online* 26, no. 5 (2002):64-68.

Sax, Linda J., Shannon K. Gilmartin, and Alyssa N. Bryant. "Assessing Response Rates and Nonresponse Bias in Web and Paper Surveys." *Research in Higher Education* 44, no. 4 (2003):409-432.

Schuman, Howard and Stanley Presser. *Questions and Answers in Attitude Surveys: Experiments on Question Form, Wording, and Context.* Thousand Oaks, Calif.: Sage Publications, 1996. First published 1981 by Academic Press.

Szelenyi, Katalin, Alyssa N. Bryant, and Jennifer A. Lindholm. "What Money Can Buy: Examining the Effects of Prepaid Monetary Incentives on Survey Response Rates Among College Students." *Educational Research and Evaluation* 11, no. 4 (2005):385-404.

Talbot, Dawn E., Gerald R. Lowell, and Kerry Martin. "From the User's Perspective—The UCSD Libraries User Survey Project." *Journal of Academic Librarianship* 24, no. 5 (1998):357-364.

Van House, Nancy, Beth T. Well, and Charles R. McClure. *Measuring Academic Library Performance: A Practical Approach.* Chicago: American Library Association, 1990.

COVER LETTER

DATE: May 5, 2006

TO: College Library Directors Participating in CLIP Notes

FROM: Doreen Kopycinski   Kim Sando
         Lehigh University   DeSales University
         E.W. Fairchild-Martindale Library   Trexler Library
         8A Packer Avenue   2755 Station Ave
         Bethlehem, PA 18015   Center Valley, PA   18034

RE: A Survey for CLIP Notes

The College Libraries Section of the Association of College and Research Libraries publishes *CLIP Notes*, a compilation of practical information collected from college and small university libraries to benefit those considering their own policies and procedures of a particular topic. As a library volunteering to participate in this collection of information for the benefit of the readers of *CLIP Notes*, you are receiving this survey for the writing of the second edition of *User Surveys in College Libraries*. We appreciate your willingness to participate.

The following survey should take approximately 10-20 minutes to complete.

If you have administered user surveys in the last five years, we would like to have a copy of them for inclusion in this upcoming *CLIP Note*. Please either send an electronic copy (attach a document, refer to a URL, etc.) by email to kas9@desales.edu or dok205@lehigh.edu or send a print copy to Kim Sando, DeSales University, Trexler Library, 2755 Station Ave., Center Valley, PA 18034.

If you have NOT administered a user survey in the last five years, we would still like to hear your feedback by completing this survey.

Thank you for your consideration of this survey—your participation is essential to the success of the *CLIP Notes* program.

PLEASE RESPOND BY JUNE 23, 2006.

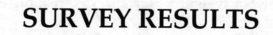

SURVEY RESULTS

1. Name of person completing the survey: (133 responses)

2. Job title of person completing survey: (133 responses)

3. Telephone number: (133 responses)

4. Email address: (133 responses)

5. Institution name and address: (133 responses)

6. Approximate FTE student enrollment at your institution: (133 responses)

1,000 or less	–	12	(9%)
1,001-2,500	–	45	(33.8%)
2,501-5,000	–	53	(39.8%)
5,001-7,500	–	16	(12%)
Over 7,500	–	7	(5.3%)

7. Number of full-time equivalent librarians: (132 responses)

1-5	–	35	(26.52%)
5.01-10	–	68	(51.52%)
10.01-15	–	23	(17.42%)
15.01-36	–	6	(4.54%)

- Mean – 8.1 FTE
- Median – 7 FTE
- Mode – 6 FTE

8. Number of full-time equivalent library support staff: (132 responses)

0-5	–	33	(25%)
5.01-10	–	49	(37%)
10.01-15	–	30	(23%)
15.01-20	–	11	(8%)
20.01-68	–	9	(7%)

- Mean – 10.4 FTE
- Median – 8.5 FTE
- Mode – 7 FTE

9. Has your library conducted at least one survey, within the past five years, that included questions about library use? (133 responses)

No – 17 (13%)

Yes – 116 (87%)

If yes, please note how many:

1	–	25	(22%)
2	–	26	(22%)
3	–	27	(23%)
4	–	14	(12%)
5	–	12	(10%)
7	–	3	(3%)
8	–	1	(1%)
10 or more	–	8	(7%)

- Mean – 3
- Median – 3
- Mode – 3

10. What types of surveys have been conducted? (check all that apply) (255 responses)

User satisfaction/dissatisfaction –	103	(40%)
Needs assessment (to determine unmet service needs) –	55	(22%)
User reactions to particular products or services –	65	(25%)
Other (please specify [noted below]): –	32	(13%)

Bibliographic Instruction/Information Literacy/Fluency - 8 responses
- Student survey - 4
- Faculty survey - 2
- General/did not specify audience - 2

Services - 4 responses

LibQUAL+™ - 4 responses

Website - 3 responses

Facility/Furniture - 2 responses

Additional Responses - 11 responses
- Identifying populations using the library…
- evaluating a cultural program
- evaluating student perceptions of the popular journal collection
- attitudinal
- Merged Information Services Organizations (MISO) Survey

- We ask what we can do better in each section of our long range strategic plan
- We use a Materials Availability Survey
- General Satisfaction Survey
- Reference Satisfaction Survey
- ISR has also done several focus group sessions with faculty and students
- We also have 4 - 5 questions attached to the campus survey 'Your First College Year' which is distributed by institutional research to first year students in the spring semester

11. What survey methods have been used? (Check all that apply) (204 responses)

Paper survey	–	64	(31%)
Focus group (a group interview conducted by an outside facilitator)	–	30	(15%)
Group interview (a group interview conducted by an in-house facilitator)	–	10	(5%)
Telephone survey	–	3	(1%)
Computer-based survey (specify the program/website used [noted below])	–	97	(48%)

Web-based Services - 61
- LibQUAL+™ - 36
- SurveyMonkey.com – 18
- MISO - 3
- Zoomerang™ - 2
- Noel-Levitz Student Satisfaction Survey - 1
- WebSurveyor - 1

Course Management Programs - 5
- Blackboard - 3
- Banner - 1
- Manhattan Course Management software - 1

Survey Software - 2
- Inquisite - 1
- Pronto Survey software - 1

Additional Responses - 29
- Web-based/online - 12
- In-house/locally produced - 9
- E-mail - 3
- Camtasia - 1

- FrontPage with Access database underneath - 1
- NSSES – 1
- Other - 2

12. Specify any other type of survey method used beyond those noted in the previous question: (6 responses)

- As part of planning for our new multi-use building, we collected user suggestions for the library and other components of the building.
- Flipchart questions in main reading room
- Informal survey on library Website: one question each week
- Web usability studies
- WebSurveyor
- Will use focus groups this fall

13. Do you offer an incentive (award, name placed in drawing, etc.) for completion of the survey(s)? (111 responses)

Yes	–	**60**	**(54%)**
No	–	**51**	**(46%)**
If yes, what	–	**91 responses**	

- iPods (incl. nano, shuffle) - 28
- Gift certificate to bookstore/Merchandise from bookstore - 11
- Gift certificate - 10
- Incentive offered but not specified in survey - 7
- Candy - 5
- Cash - 4
- Copy cards/Print credits/Money on campus card - 4
- Jump Drives/Thumb drives - 3
- Pens/Highlighters/School supplies - 3
- Book scholarship/Coupon for free book out of the college book sale - 2
- Gift cards - 2
- Gift cards/coupons from coffee shop - 2
- Pizza drawing - 2
- Refreshments - 2
- Coupons, etc. from local merchants - 1
- DVD player - 1
- Movie tickets - 1
- Mugs - 1
- PDAs - 1
- Stuffed toys – 1

14. Why were these surveys undertaken (check all that apply)? (549 responses)

To improve programs/services –	102	(18.6%)
To provide evidence of student attitudes or feelings –	81	(14.8%)
For accreditation purposes –	53	(9.7%)
To respond to student concerns –	47	(8.6%)
For general feedback--no specific purpose in mind –	44	(8.0%)
To establish usage patterns –	43	(7.8%)
To help staff make informed decisions about purchases –	38	(6.9%)
To inform users about services –	37	(6.7%)
To establish a case for new services –	25	(4.6%)
As part of a mandated program review –	19	(3.5%)
To plan for a new building –	16	(2.9%)
To determine services to be dropped –	14	(2.6%)
Request from institutional administration –	11	(2.0%)
To gather feedback from users to incorporate into personnel evaluations –	3	(0.5%)
Other (please specify [noted below]) –	16	(2.9%)

- Assist in library website design
- At the time (2002), we were really interested in whether our students were using our various databases and our online catalog or were instead relying on the web. Most picked a search engine.
- Customer satisfaction
- Define satisfaction & importance of collections
- Determine feasibility for a major cooperative project
- Evaluate a cultural program
- General assessment
- Part of assessment process for units in the university
- Improvement in information literacy after the first year general education courses
- Plan first year instruction in information fluency
- Instructional session feedback
- Journal subscriptions
- Learn how students and faculty members are using the library, what their demands are and what their satisfaction level is with current services, so we may design new services & revise current in response
- Plan for classroom
- Plan for renovation and expansion

15. Check what additional resources (if any) that you made use of for your survey (check all that apply): (128 responses)

None	–	60	(47%)
A campus consultant	–	20	(16%)
Additional institutional staffing	–	9	(7%)
Volunteers from outside the library	–	8	(6%)
Additional institutional funding	–	7	(5%)
Grant funding	–	5	(4%)
An outside consultant	–	5	(4%)
Other (please specify [noted below])	–	14	(11%)

- Campus departments (Institutional Research/Data Mining/ Computer Services/Web Development/ Information Technology/Communications - 4
- Library Faculty Committee/Teaching faculty/Faculty focus groups - 3
- LibQUAL+™ - 2
- Inter-institutional collaboration - 1
- Strategic planning group - 1
- Students in a new polling methodology class wrote, administered, and analyzed the poll - 1
- Support from Friends of the Library and from OhioLINK - 1
- Surveys shared by colleagues - 1

16. The survey was written by (check all that apply): (150 responses)

One staff member, with input from others	–	46	(31%)
One staff member	–	4	(3%)
A group of staff members	–	44	(29%)
Other (please specify [noted below])	–	56	(37%)

- LibQUAL+™ - 20
- Outsourced -6
- Adapted from another survey – 4
- Campus library committee/non-library faculty – 4
- Library staff and consultant – 4
- ARL – 2
- Inter-institutional effort – 2
- MISO – 2
- Students from a Polling/Social Research Methods class – 2
- Librarians and Dean/IR staff – 2
- ACRL -1
- OhioLINK -1

- Focus groups done by grad student, faculty and library committee -1
- Noel-Levitz -1
- Part of general campus NSSI -1
- Standardized instrument -1
- State statistics office -1
- Texas A&M Faculty -1

17. The survey was distributed by (check all that apply): (131 responses)

One staff member, with help from others –	37	(28%)
One staff member –	14	(11%)
A group of staff members –	35	(27%)
Other (please specify [noted below]) –	45	(34%)

- Campus department (Institutional Research/Information Technology/Institutional Effectiveness/Student Services, etc.) - 11
- Electronically/online - 8
- Web (announcement on library's website, SurveyMonkey.com, etc.) - 8
- E-mail - 3
- Students (library assistants/class project) - 3
- Associate Dean - 2
- Faculty (in classes, members of library committee, etc.) - 2
- Computer terminal in library - 2
- LibQUAL+™ - 2
- ARL - 1
- Focus groups done by grad student - 1
- Paper - 1
- Vendor - 1

18. The method of distribution was (check all that apply): (191 responses)

By e-mail –	71	(37%)
Place at service point –	44	(23%)
By campus mail –	22	(12%)
Other (please specify [noted below]) –	54	(28%)

- Distributed during classes - 13
- Web-based - 11
- Focus group discussion - 6
- Online - 5
- Various campus locations (student center/dining hall/computer lab) - 5
- Blackboard/Manhattan course management systems - 3
- Telephone - 2

- Asking students who walk in the door - 1
- At campus gatherings - 1
- Computer workstation interactive program - 1
- Electronic at end of on-line registration process - 1
- Faculty meeting - 1
- Given to department chairs for distribution to faculty - 1
- Orientation sessions - 1
- Paper copies available in library - 1
- SurveyMonkey.com - 1

19. Results of the survey were compiled by (check all that apply): (149 responses)

One staff member, with help from others –	45	(30%)
One staff member –	25	(17%)
A group of staff members –	15	(10%)
Campus office outside the library –	26	(17%)
Other (please specify [noted below]) –	38	(26%)

- LibQUAL+™ - 19
- ARL - 3
- Students (team from the polling class/graduate students) - 3
- Outsourced - 2
- ACRL - 1
- Group of staff members from participating institutions - 1
- Library committee - 1
- MISO - 1
- Noel-Levitz - 1
- Office of focus group leader - 1
- Software - 1
- Southeast Research Associations - 1
- State statistics office - 1
- Survey services staff - 1
- Vendor - 1

20. Which of the following resources did you find MOST useful in developing your survey (check only one)? (113 responses)

Used no resources –	34	(30%)
Articles from library literature –	29	(26%)
CLIP Notes' *User Surveys in College Libraries* (1995) –	9	(8%)
Literature from other disciplines (e.g. business, –	5	(4%)

sociology, etc.)		
Books written for librarians –	3	**(3%)**
SPEC kits from the Association of Research Libraries –	1	**(1%)**
Other (please specify [noted below]) –	32	**(28%)**

- Sample surveys/surveys from other libraries - 10
- Comments/ideas/needs by users and staff - 3
- LibQUAL+™ (materials/ALA sessions)- 3
- Library's previous survey/experience - 3
- Consultant - 2
- Faculty (research/statistics/management/social sciences) - 2
- Institutional Research staff - 2
- ACRL/OLMS course - 1
- Course work in statistical methods - 1
- Expertise among participating institutions - 1
- Expertise of IR staff - 1
- MSA guidelines - 1
- Other peer institutions - 1
- Uncertain. Survey opened before I got here. - 1

21. If you remember the title of a specific source that you found exceptionally useful, please list it: (6 responses)

- ACRL Information Literacy Standards
- Assessment in College Library Instruction Programs [CLIP Note #32]
- LibQUAL+™
- Measuring Library Service Quality
- too many to mention, although the work of Don Dillman is of interest
- University of Washington 2004 undergraduate library and information use survey

22. Check any campus expertise (if any) you used for your surveys (check all that apply): (150 responses)

Faculty or staff member with survey research experience –	**44**	**(29%)**
A campus unit that provides survey assistance –	**39**	**(26%)**
None –	**29**	**(19%)**
Institutional computer center –	**22**	**(15%)**
Students enrolled in course concerned with surveys –	**9**	**(6%)**
Other (please specify [noted below]) –	**7**	**(5%)**

- WebSurveyor Instructor
- Other Librarian Input

- Human subject review committee
- Library Faculty Advisory Committee
- Staff member has studied and audited courses, gone to workshops regarding assessment and statistics
- Members of Library Committee
- Campus data miner and web developer

23. Did the results of the survey provide you with useful information? (110 responses)

Very useful information –	43	(39.1%)
Useful information –	52	(47.3%)
Somewhat useful information –	14	(12.7%)
Not very useful information –	1	(0.9%)
No useful information –	0	(0%)

24. What was done with the results (check all that apply)? (412 responses)

Comments circulated among library staff –	97	(23.5%)
Changes made in services and/or staffing –	72	(17.5%)
Results shared with library committee –	71	(17.2%)
Report written for institutional administration –	67	(16.3%)
Changes made in policies and/or procedures –	48	(11.7%)
Changes made in purchasing decisions –	22	(5.3%)
Incorporated into personnel evaluations –	7	(1.7%)
Nothing –	1	(0.2%)
Other (please specify [noted below]) –	27	(6.6%)

- Changes in IL teaching approaches
- Changes made in content of first-year introductory sessions
- Results used in making the case for improvements in the library facility
- The students all hate the library furniture, so we set up a joint committee with some of them and some staff members to make recommendations for new furniture.
- Changes to website design
- No changes made in existing policy on library hours for the weekend
- Report in progress
- Results shared with administration
- article for campus newspaper/library newsletter - 3
- Reported to the campus via web page
- Incorporated into annual report
- Used for external review

- Comparisons made over 5-10 year period
- Used in writing our strategic plan
- Results/survey data used in many different ways: e.g. annual assessment report, justification for purchase requests, annual report, etc.
- Used for budget justification
- Used to develop operational plan for next A.Y.
- Respond to requests - such as a demonstration of electronic resources. Changes would be made in services and policies if indicated they were needed

25. How satisfied were you with the process you used? (110 responses)

Very satisfied	–	31	**(28.2%)**
Satisfied	–	64	**(58.2%)**
Neither satisfied nor unsatisfied	–	12	**(10.9%)**
Dissatisfied	–	3	**(2.7%)**
Very dissatisfied	–	0	**(0%)**

26. Check all the problems that occurred: (189 responses)

Low number of responses received	–	49	**(25.9%)**
Figuring out how to get the survey to both library users and non users	–	36	**(19.0%)**
After reviewing responses, realized that some questions were not needed	–	22	**(11.6%)**
After reviewing responses, realized that important questions were NOT asked	–	19	**(10.1%)**
People responded to questions differently from what was expected	–	16	**(8.5%)**
Survey results gave no new information	–	11	**(5.8%)**
Lack of support from college administration	–	5	**(2.6%)**
Low staff cooperation	–	1	**(0.5%)**
Other (please specify [noted below])	–	30	**(15.9%)**

- When using email to distribute survey, many emails bounced back because students exceeded their disk quotas either on campus or off-campus with another email provider; this impacted response rate.
- Some blank surveys turned in to get chance at cash award.
- Realized that some questions were misunderstood and should have been worded better
- Survey methodology is frustrating to some respondents

- One of the surveys got very little response. The faculty survey gave little new information. The student focus groups were most helpful.
- Low number of responses for online survey only
- Survey questions were not answered realistically, but rather how they thought about themselves.
- Campus policy on bulk email notification was a major hassle.
- Every year we review and update the survey to avoid or correct the problems listed above.
- I wanted to sort answers by year in school but was not able to, which made tracking learning over time impossible.
- There were 81 responses, which is low, but the results pinpointed a trend, which was very useful (reliance on web over library).
- Expanded survey needed
- The questions were the "same-old, same-old"
- There may have been some duplication, although we indicated on the survey that if the person had already taken the survey in another class, he/she should not take it again
- Some confusion on the part of our distance learning students in how to respond to some survey statements
- Faculty unhappy to spend class time conducting survey

27. What advice would you give to another librarian planning a survey? (62 total responses)

Keep it Simple
- Focus on one or two concerns
- Keep survey short and question tightly focused
- Provide a clear concise idea of what it is you need want to evaluate

Be sure to plan and test
- Give yourself a long planning time
- Start early, plan carefully
- Do some testing, be sure the questions reflect what you want to find out
- Test especially your wording/terminology/acronyms and initialisms, provide comment box
- Test a survey instrument first
- Administer to library student workers first and evaluate

Use SurveyMonkey.com, LibQUAL+™
- Our 11 item SurveyMonkey.com survey from the previous year gave us equally good results
- LibQUAL+™ is a product that has been tested and validated
- Use LibQUAL+™ at least once every five years

Seek expert help
- If you're not trained as a social science researcher, ask for help
- Consult with others outside the library who have expertise in this area
- Make use of your institution's research unit if possible

Publicize, market and communicate results
- Be sure you actually use the information gathered
- Market it...especially in university publications
- Publicize the changes made as a result of the survey

28. Permission to publish documents (check one of the following): (109 responses, 39 of which gave permission to publish)

29. To the best of your knowledge, check the statement that most closely describes your library's status on surveys: (17 responses)

We have conducted surveys/ a survey in the past but one has not been conducted within the past five years	11	**(65%)**
We have never conducted a survey	6	**(35%)**

30. What reasons have prevented your institution from conducting any or additional surveys (check all that apply): (20 responses)

Lack of staff time	8	**(40%)**
Most issues are pretty well understood/ survey not necessary	4	**(20%)**
Skeptical about the benefit of surveys	2	**(10%)**
Lack of funding	0	**(0%)**
Lack of expertise (in formulating and conduction survey	0	**(0%)**
Never found anything we needed to survey	0	**(0%)**
Other (please specify [noted below])	6	**(30%)**

- We have hosted informal focus groups for feedback because this mode seems more consistent with our organizational culture. However, we have created a survey that we will undertake next semester.
- There are library questions on university-wide student surveys
- I honestly cannot remember if I have done any of your surveys.
- Administrative turnover
- President questioned faculty status of librarians so previously identified priorities, including assessment efforts, had to be delayed to respond to attack on faculty status.
- We do LOTS of assessment of student learning. We find that much more valuable than "smile sheets."

DOCUMENTS

FACULTY SURVEYS

PORTER HENDERSON LIBRARY
FACULTY SURVEY
Spring 2005

1.   What is your present classification?

☐Adjunct   ☐Instructor   ☐Lecturer   ☐Asst. Prof.   ☐Assoc. Prof.   ☐Prof.

2.   In which of the following colleges or school do you teach?

☐ Business & Professional Studies   ☐Education   ☐Liberal and Fine Arts ☐Sciences

_____Department

3.   Tenure Status.

☐Tenured   ☐Tenure-track   ☐Non-tenure position

4.   Please indicate how satisfied you are with the following Library services and resources. (USE THE FOLLOWING SCALE FOR EACH ITEM LISTED: 5=VERY SATISFIED, 4=SOMEWHAT SATISFIED, 3=NEUTRAL, 2=SOMEWHAT DISSATISFIED, 1=VERY DISSATISFIED, X=NEVER USED.)

RamNet___   RamCat___   RamCOPS___   Reference Services___

Media Services___   Circulation Services___   Course Reserves Services___

Interlibrary Loan___   Weekday Hours___   Weekend Hours___   Summer Hours___

Signs & Directions___

Comments:_____

_____

_____

(FOR QUESTIONS 5-6, PLEASE USE A SCALE OF 5=ONCE A WEEK OR MORE, 4=ONCE EVERY TWO OR THREE WEEKS, 3=ONCE A MONTH, 2=ONCE OR TWICE A SEMESTER, 1=NEVER.)

5.   Please indicate how often you access either RamCat and/or RamNet from

Library___ Home___ Office___   Other___: Please specify_____

6.   How often do you need to seek assistance with your research from

Librarians___ Colleagues on campus___ Colleagues off-campus___ Others___: Please specify_____

[Please turn over and complete page 2.]

Indicate the extent to which you agree or disagree with the following statements. (USE THE FOLLOWING SCALE AND CIRCLE ONE RESPONSE FOR EACH STATEMENT: 5=STRONGLY AGREE, 4=AGREE, 3=NEUTRAL, 2=DISAGREE, 1=STRONGLY DISAGREE, X=DON'T KNOW.)

7. RamCat (Online Catalog) is easy to use.
    5   4   3   2   1   X

8. RAMNET has the databases I need to complete my research.
    5   4   3   2   1   X

9. The Library's resources meet my research needs.
    5   4   3   2   1   X

10. The Reference Desk staff members provide knowledgeable assistance for your information needs.
    5   4   3   2   1   X

11. The Reference Desk staff members provide friendly service.
    5   4   3   2   1   X

12. The Circulation Desk staff members provide competent assistance with your Library transactions.
    5   4   3   2   1   X

13. The Circulation Desk staff members provide friendly service.
    5   4   3   2   1   X

14. The Library's WEB pages are helpful.
    5   4   3   2   1   X

15. Classes with library instruction and/or that use one of the Library's tutorials are helpful.
    5   4   3   2   1   X

Comments: for Questions 7-15_____

_____

_____

_____

What specific improvements would you suggest for the Library's information services and resources?

_____

_____

_____

_____

Ferrum College

1. Rate how well you think the library's collections support the academic needs of your students.

    Very Poorly   Very Well
    1   2   3   4   5

2. Rate your own understanding of the scope of the library's electronic resources.

    Poor   Very Good
    1   2   3   4   5

3. What do you see as the library's key strengths related to supporting student research, and how can these strengths be improved?

    _____
    _____
    _____
    _____
    _____
    _____
    _____
    _____
    _____

4. Please list problems and concerns students have expressed to you concerning the library.

    _____
    _____
    _____
    _____
    _____
    _____
    _____
    _____

5. Please rate the Media Center collection, equipment, and facilities.

    Very poor   Average   Very good
    1   2   3   4   5

6. Please list aspects of our Media service you find most successful. Also, are there areas that need improvement?

    _____
    _____
    _____
    _____
    _____
    _____
    _____

7. Do you find media funding adequate for your division or department?
    Yes   No

8. What new library or media resources would you like to see?

_____
_____
_____
_____

9. Please rate your own ability to find and use library resources at Ferrum.

Poor   Average   Very Good
 1   2   3   4   5

10. Please check the materials you use frequently. Please circle the two types you use most often.

_____Books

_____Magazines and journals (print)

_____Reference books

_____Full text databases

_____Electronic books

_____Online magazines

_____Online indexes

_____Online reference books

_____Microfilm

_____Electronic reserves

11. Do you think having to pay for interlibrary loans inhibits student research?

        Yes   No

        Does it inhibit your own research?

        Yes   No

2002 LIBRARY FACULTY SURVEY

I.   General Information

1.1   Academic department _____

1.2   How many years have you been at Furman?

a_____ 0-5   d_____ 16-20
b_____ 6-10   e_____ 21-25
c_____ 11-15   f_____ More than 25

1.3   Which campus libraries have you used during this academic year? Check all that apply.

a_____ James B. Duke Library (main)   d_____ Education Curriculum Lab
b_____ Maxwell Music Library   e_____ Other—please specify
c_____ Ezell Science Reading Room

1.4   Besides the Furman libraries, to which (if any) other libraries have you gone for class preparation or professional research during the past year? Check all that apply.

a_____ I have not gone to any other libraries to do class preparation or professional research

b_____ Clemson University Library   e_____ University of South Carolina Library
c_____ Greenville County Public Library   f_____ Other—please specify:
d_____ Greenville Hospital Library

1.5   In an average year, how many of your courses include a paper or other assignment that requires use of library resources on the part of your students?

a_____ None   d_____ Three
b_____ One   e_____ Four
c_____ Two   f_____ Five

II.   Library Resources

2.1   What kinds of library resources have you used for class preparation during the current academic year? Check all that apply.

a_____ Books   g_____ Online periodicals/journals
b_____ Books on tape   h_____ Print periodicals/journals
c_____ Electronic books   i_____ Reference sources
d_____ Government documents   j_____ Research databases
e_____ Music CD's   k_____ Videos, DVD's, etc.
f_____ Music scores   l_____ Other—please specify:

2.2   What kinds of library resources have you used for research during the current academic year? Check all that apply.

a_____ Books   g_____ Online periodicals/journals
b_____ Books on tape   h_____ Print periodicals/journals
c_____ Electronic books   i_____ Reference sources
d_____ Government documents   j_____ Research databases
e_____ Music CD's   k_____ Videos, DVD's, etc.
f_____ Music scores   l_____ Other—please specify:

2.3   If the library's budget increases in the future, what kinds of resources do you believe should be the highest priorities for new acquisitions? Choose up to three, and rank your choices as #1, #2, and #3.

a_____ Books   g_____ Online periodicals/journals
b_____ Books on tape   h_____ Print periodicals/journals
c_____ Electronic books   i_____ Reference sources
d_____ Government documents   j_____ Research databases
e_____ Music CD's   k_____ Videos, DVD's, etc.
f_____ Music scores   l_____ Other—please specify:

2.4   Comments on library resources:

III.   **Library Services**

3.1   Have you ever had a librarian teach a library research instruction session for one of your classes?

A_____ Yes   b_____ No (if no, skip to question 3.5)

3.2   How many of your courses include a library instruction session during a typical year?

a_____ None   d_____ Three
b_____ One   e_____ Four
c_____ Two   f_____ Five

3.3   How helpful have you found library research instruction sessions to be for your students?

a_____ Very helpful   d_____ Not very helpful
b_____ Helpful   e_____ Not at all helpful
c_____ Somewhat helpful   f_____ Don't know

3.4   What have you found to be the most helpful component of library research instruction sessions?

3.5   What could be done to improve library research instruction sessions in your discipline?

Please indicate the degree to which you agree with each of the following statements regarding library services:

1 Strongly Agree	2 Agree	3 Neutral	4 Disagree	5 Strongly Disagree

3.6	Reference desk hours are convenient.	1	2	3	4	5
3.7	Librarians and library staff are efficient, helpful, and courteous.	1	2	3	4	5
3.8	Library student workers are efficient, helpful, and courteous.	1	2	3	4	5
3.9	Interlibrary loan services are timely and useful.	1	2	3	4	5
3.10	The items I need are usually on the shelf where I expect to find them.	1	2	3	4	5

3.11   Comments on Library Services:

IV.   Online Resources

4.1   Have you used the Furman library website for research?

a_____ Yes   b_____ No (if no, skip to question 4.5)

4.2   How helpful have you found the library website in your research?

a_____ Very helpful   d_____ Not very helpful
b_____ Helpful   e_____ Not at all helpful
c_____ Somewhat helpful

4.3   How easy/difficult have you found the library website to use?

a_____ Very easy   d_____ Difficult
b_____ Easy   e_____ Very difficult
c_____ Somewhat difficult

4.4   What could be added to or changed about the library website to make it more useful for your students or for your research?

Raugust Library
Library Satisfaction Questionnaire – Faculty

April, 2006

The library staff is constantly trying to improve library services for the students and faculty. Please help us by completing this questionnaire and returning it to the library by May 5. Many thanks!

Optional: **What is your department?** _____

1. **How often to you come to the library?**

   _____ Daily
   _____ Several times a week
   _____ Once a week
   _____ Once a month
   _____ Once a semester
   _____ Never

2. **Why do you come to the library? Check all that apply.**

   _____ Research
   _____ Check out materials from the collection
   _____ Return materials
   _____ Put an item on reserve
   _____ Watch a video
   _____ Listen to a cassette, record, or cd
   _____ Attend a library instruction class
   _____ Use a public computer workstation
   _____ Photocopy
   _____ Group meeting
   _____ Request or pick up an interlibrary loan item
   _____ Check out av equipment

3. **Were you greeted promptly and courteously at the circulation desk?**

   _____ yes
   _____ no

4. **How satisfied are you with the help you receive, on average, at the circulation desk?**

   Most satisfied   Least satisfied

   ___ 5   ___ 4   ___ 3   ___ 2   ___ 1

5. **Are the checkout periods for materials adequate for faculty use?**

    _____ yes
    _____ no

6. **Are the checkout periods for materials adequate for student use?**

    _____ yes
    _____ no

7. **Have you ever used ODIN, the online catalog?**

    _____ yes
    _____ no

8. **Did you find it fairly easy to use?**

    _____ yes
    _____ no   Describe any problem:

9. **In general, are you able to find the book or other material on the shelf, once you have identified what you need?**

    _____ yes
    _____ no

10. **How satisfied are you with the *number* of public access terminals in the library?**

    Most satisfied   Least satisfied

    ___5   ___4   ___3   ___2   ___1

11. **How satisfied are you with the *quality* of the public access terminals in the library?**

    Most satisfied   Least satisfied

    ___5   ___4   ___3   ___2   ___1

12. Have you accessed the library homepage from off campus?

    _____ yes
    _____ no

13. If yes to question 12, did you have any problems with access?

    _____ yes **Describe:**
    _____ no

14. Are you aware of the link from the library homepage to an online resources page for your discipline?

    _____ yes
    _____ no

15. Check off all the services which you have used from the Indexes and Databases page.

_____ Academic Search Premier
_____ Ancestry
_____ Business Source Premier
_____ CINAHL
_____ CIOS
_____ Classical Music Library
_____ Clinical Pharmacology
_____ Contemporary Authors
_____ Encyclopedia Britannica
_____ ERIC
_____ FirstSearch
_____ GPO Access
_____ Health Source: Nursing/Academic Edition
_____ JSTOR
_____ LaND (Library Access North Dakota)
_____ Literature Online (LION)
_____ MasterFILE Premier
_____ Medline
_____ National Newspapers
_____ netLibrary
_____ North Dakota Statistical Abstract
_____ OCLC WorldCat
_____ Opposing Viewpoints
_____ Oxford English Dictionary
_____ Pre-CINAHL
_____ Proquest Education Journals
_____ Proquest Psychology Journals

_____ PsychInfo
_____ Regional Business News
_____ Thomson Micromedex

16. How satisfied are you with the SCOPE AND VARIETY of these online resources?

Most satisfied   Least satisfied

___ 5   ___ 4   ___ 3   ___ 2   ___ 1

17. What other online resources would you like to add to the library's collection?

18. Have you ever read an ebook from netLibrary?

_____ yes
_____ no

19. If yes, how easy did you find netLibrary to use?

Most difficult   Least difficult

___ 5   ___ 4   ___ 3   ___ 2   ___ 1

20. Have you ever downloaded or printed a full-text article from JSTOR or any other full-text database?

_____ yes
_____ no

21. If yes, how easy did you find the process of downloading or printing?

Most difficult   Least difficult

___ 5   ___ 4   ___ 3   ___ 2   ___ 1

22. How satisfied are you with the BOOK collection in your discipline?

Most satisfied   Least satisfied

___ 5   ___ 4   ___ 3   ___ 2   ___ 1

23. How satisfied are you with the JOURNAL collection in your discipline?

Most satisfied   Least satisfied

___ 5   ___ 4   ___ 3   ___ 2   ___ 1

24. How satisfied are you with the AV collection in your discipline?

Most satisfied   Least satisfied

___ 5   ___ 4   ___ 3   ___ 2   ___ 1

25. How satisfied are you with the library's hours?

Most satisfied   Least satisfied

___ 5   ___ 4   ___ 3   ___ 2   ___ 1

26. If dissatisfied with the library's hours, how would you change them?

27. Have you used interlibrary loan at Raugust Library?

_____ yes
_____ no

28. If yes, how satisfied are you with this service?

Most satisfied   Least satisfied

___ 5   ___ 4   ___ 3   ___ 2   ___ 1

29. If yes, how long did it take (on average) for you to receive your loans?

_____ hours
_____ 1 day
_____ 2 days
_____ 3 days
_____ 1 week
_____ 2 weeks
_____ never

30. Have you ever used the Ariel service for interlibrary loans?
_____ yes
_____ no
_____ not sure

31. If yes, how satisfied are you with this service?

Most satisfied   Least satisfied

___ 5   ___ 4   ___ 3   ___ 2   ___ 1

32. Have you ever consulted a reference librarian at Raugust Library?

_____ yes
_____ no

33. If yes, how satisfied are you with this service?

Most satisfied   Least satisfied

___ 5   ___ 4   ___ 3   ___ 2   ___ 1

34. Have you ever requested a session in library use or other instruction from a librarian at Raugust Library for your students?

_____ yes
_____ no

35. If yes, how satisfied are you with this instruction?

Most satisfied   Least satisfied

___ 5   ___ 4   ___ 3   ___ 2   ___ 1

36. Did the instruction occur in the library or in your classroom during a class period?

_____ library
_____ classroom

37. How comfortable do you find the library on average?

Most comfortable   Least comfortable

___ 5   ___ 4   ___ 3   ___ 2   ___ 1

38. How would you change the library's furniture or arrangement?

39. Other comments:

Thank you for your time and input!

Phyllis Ann K. Bratton
Director, Raugust Library

Lander University

ANNUAL FACULTY SURVEY OF LIBRARY

2005-2006

Indicate your department: Art

If you have no comments on the library, please check here ○ . Then go to the bottom of the screen and press Submit.

A. Please indicate how you make use of the library and its resources:
1. Reading journals/newspapers Often or daily
2. Researching Often or daily
3. Preparing for lectures Often or daily
4. Using interlibrary loan services Often or daily
5. Using electronic periodical indexes (like InfoTrac/DISCUS) Often or daily
6. Using electronic periodical indexes from your office Often or daily
7. Using the online catalog Often or daily
8. Using the online catalog from your office Often or daily
9. Using the e-book collection Often or daily
10. Browsing in the book stacks Often or daily
11. Borrowing materials Often or daily
12. Reading for pleasure Often or daily
13. Java City (coffee shop) Often or daily

B. Please indicate your satisfaction with the library staff and facilities:
1. Circulation desk services very satisfied
2. Reference desk services very satisfied
3. Library instructional services very satisfied
4. Interlibrary loan services very satisfied
5. Physical facilities very satisfied
6. Noise level in the library very satisfied
7. Library hours very satisfied

C. Please indicate your opinion of the following statements·
1. I make assignments that require library research. strongly agree
2. I am comfortable retrieving and using information electronically. strongly agree
3. The Internet has changed the way I locate information. strongly agree
4. Lander students are being given the instructional and reference services they need. strongly agree
5. I encourage my students to use the subscription periodical indexes (like InfoTrac) which are available through the library.
strongly agree
6. I would like to have one of the librarians come to my office to demonstrate electronic resources. If you would like this, please put your name in the comments box or email me ahare@lander.edu. strongly agree
7. I am comfortable using the Lander Library's web site for accessing information. strongly agree
8. Java City (coffee shop) is an asset to the Library. strongly agree

9. I encourage my students to use the book collection.   strongly agree

Any comments? If you want a response, be sure to include your name and e-mail address or phone number.

Submit   Reset

2005 Siena College Faculty Survey on Library Services and Resources:
Please take a few minutes to fill out this survey

School: □ Business   □ Liberal Arts   □ Science
Dept:

Status: □ full-time   □ part-time

Please indicate which the following library services you have utilized during the last two years:
□ borrowing books   □ borrowing videos and compact discs   □ interlibrary loan services
□ ConnectNY   □ print reserves   □ electronic reserves
□ library instruction   □ rush cataloging (priority processing)   □ reference assistance
□ database searching   □ assisting with new course proposals   □ faculty study carrels
□ Direct Access card   □ borrowing AV equipment
□ recommending books for the collection   □ *Choice* cards

Please assess the following <u>library services</u>, as a faculty member:

Reference assistance to students
                          □ very good   □ good □ satisfactory   □ fair   □ not sure
Hours available for studying and research
                          □ very good   □ good □ satisfactory   □ fair   □ not sure
Handling book requests   □ very good   □ good □ satisfactory   □ fair   □ not sure

Interlibrary loan   □ very good   □ good □ satisfactory   □ fair   □ not sure
ConnectNY   □ very good   □ good □ satisfactory   □ fair   □ not sure

Audiovisual equipment delivery and setup
                          □ very good   □ good □ satisfactory   □ fair   □ not sure

EEC support for projectors and sound systems
                          □ very good   □ good □ satisfactory   □ fair   □ not sure

Electronic reserves   □ very good   □ good □ satisfactory   □ fair   □ not sure

Print reserves   □ very good   □ good □ satisfactory   □ fair   □ not sure

Library instruction   □ very good   □ good □ satisfactory   □ fair   □ not sure

Comments:

Please assess the following <u>library resources</u>, from the perspective of a faculty member in your <u>discipline</u>:

Book collection	☐ very good	☐ good	☐ satisfactory	☐Fair	☐ not sure
Print journals	☐ very good	☐ good	☐ satisfactory	☐Fair	☐ not sure
Electronic journals	☐ very good	☐ good	☐ satisfactory	☐Fair	☐ not sure
Reference books	☐ very good	☐ good	☐ satisfactory	☐Fair	☐ not sure
Research databases	☐ very good	☐ good	☐ satisfactory	☐Fair	☐ not sure
Special collections	☐ very good	☐ good	☐ satisfactory	☐Fair	☐ not sure
Videos	☐ very good	☐ good	☐ satisfactory	☐Fair	☐ not sure
Internet resources	☐ very good	☐ good	☐ satisfactory	☐Fair	☐ not sure

Comments:

Please answer these questions about the Library Web site:

How often do you use the Library Web site?
　☐ Daily　　☐ A few times weekly　　☐ Weekly　　☐ Monthly　　☐ Infrequently

Do you use the following Library Web pages from home?
Library Home page:	☐ yes	☐ no
CYRIL:	☐ yes	☐ no
Research databases	☐ yes	☐ no
Do you know how to use EZ-Proxy?	☐ yes	☐ no

How do you use the Library Web site?
　☐　To search CYRIL, the Web on-line catalog
　☐　To search the research databases
　☐　To retrieve electronic journal articles
　☐　To order interlibrary loans
　☐　To use ConnectNY
　☐　To use reference email
　☐　To find out Library hours
　☐　To learn what is new at the Library

How would you rate the Library Web?
General organization	☐ very good	☐ good	☐ Sat.	☐ Fair	☐ not sure
Ease of use	☐ very good	☐ good	☐ Sat.	☐ Fair	☐ not sure
Searching CYRIL	☐ very good	☐ good	☐ Sat.	☐ Fair	☐ not sure
Finding appropriate database	☐ very good	☐ good	☐ Sat.	☐ Fair	☐ not sure
Forms (ILL, reference, etc.)	☐ very good	☐ good	☐ Sat.	☐ Fair	☐ not sure

In which area(s) of the Library, could our services or resources be improved?

St. John Fisher College
Lavery Library Focus Group
Faculty Questions

General:

How would you describe your ideal library?

What's been your own experience using Lavery library?

Resources, Functionality, Assistance with your research, Assistance with student research.

Access to Information:

What are your biggest impediments to acessing information in Lavery?

How might we minimize or remove these impediments?

Number of materials, quality of materials, access to materials, availability of materials.

What other resources do you use?

How does library technology help your work? Hinder it? How might the technology be improved?

Personal Control:

How readily are you able to access information through the library on your own?

What specific problems have you encountered? What tools do you miss?

What are the barriers to communicating requests for information?

What prevents people from using the library fully?

Technological, Physical, Temporal, Other.

Library as Place:

How comfortable are you with the setting and facilities of the library? What specific things contribute to your comfort?

What do your students tell you about their use of the library? How comfortable are they using it . . .?

For Research, Studying, Group projects, Other.

Affect of Service:

What issues have you had with the service in the library?

What issues have your students had with the service in the library?

What relationship should faculty have with library staff? What types of assistance do you request from the library staff?

Tisch Library Faculty Survey 2006

N = , Response Rate =

Please take a few minutes to complete the following survey. In years past the responses from the survey have led to positive changes in Tisch Library.

1. What is your academic department?

Africa & the New World	
American Studies	
Anthropology	
Art and Art History	
Asian Studies	
Biology	
Biomedical Engineering	
Boston School of Occupational Therapy	
Center for Interdisciplinary Studies	
Chemical & Biological Engineering	
Chemistry	
Child Development	
Civil & Environmental Engineering	
Classics	
Community Health	
Comparative Religion	
Computer Science	
Drama & Dance	
Economics	
Education	
Electrical & Computer Engineering	
English	
Environmental Studies	
Geology	
German, Russian & Asian Languages & Literatures	
History	
International Relations Program	
Latin American Studies	
Mathematics	
Mechanical Engineering	
Museum Studies (Visual & Critical Studies)	
Music	
Peace and Justice Studies	
Philosophy	
Physical Education/Athletics	
Physics & Astronomy	
Political Science	
Psychology	
Romance Languages	
Sociology	
Urban & Environmental Policy	
Women's Studies	
World Civilizations	
Other, please specify	

Tufts University

2. How often do you come to the Tisch Library?

Never	
Just During Exams	
1-2 Times Per Semester	
1-2 Times Per Month	
1-2 Times Per Week	
3-4 Times Per Week	
Daily	

3. How often do you access the library resources from outside Tisch using the web?

Never	
Just During Exams	
1-2 Times Per Semester	
1-2 Times Per Month	
1-2 Times Per Week	
3-4 Times Per Week	
Daily	

4. How often do you use Interlibrary Loan (ILLiad) or the Virtual Catalog to request materials from other non-Tufts libraries?

Never	
Just During Exams	
1-2 Times Per Semester	
1-2 Times Per Month	
1-2 Times Per Week	
3-4 Times Per Week	
Daily	

5. How often do you go to other non-Tufts libraries to use materials?

Never	
Just During Exams	
1-2 Times Per Semester	
1-2 Times Per Month	
1-2 Times Per Week	
3-4 Times Per Week	
Daily	

6. Do you find that the Tisch Library building hours meet your needs?

Yes	
Usually	
Sometimes	
No	

7. Please indicate your satisfaction with the following Tisch services:

	Did not know about this service	Satisfied	Dissatisfied	Do not use
Requesting materials from other libraries through ILLiad				
Requesting books through the Boston Library Consortium Virtual Catalog				
Finding e-journals				
Finding electronic databases				
Renewing books and other materials online				
Recommending an item for purchase online				
Study Space				
Photocopiers				
Reference Desk				
Reserve Services				
Media Center				
Microforms & Current Periodical Desk				
Workshops/Library instruction given in the Library's Electronic Resource Center				
Library's Collections (books, videos, journals, etc.)				

8. Please indicate your satisfaction with the Tisch Library computers (not including the Mark lab):

	Did not know about this service	Satisfied	Dissatisfied	Do not use
Internet computers				
E-mail computers				
Computers with MS-Office				
Collaborative Workstation Computer				

9. Additional Comments:

York College of Pennsylvania

Schmidt Library
Faculty Use Survey

Spring 2005

As part of our annual outcomes assessment program, we are gathering information on user satisfaction with collections, services, facilities, instruction, staff, and hours. So we can better serve your needs, please take a few minutes to answer these questions. Please return the survey to Raeann Waltersdorf via campus mail or drop your questionnaire at the Circulation Services Desk by **February 27**. Thank you.

1. In evaluating Schmidt Library, how would you rate our

Services

☐ Excellent   ☐ Very Good   ☐ Good   ☐ Fair   ☐ Poor   ☐ Unable to rate

Comments _____
_____

_____

Schmidt Library Web/Online Systems

☐ Excellent   ☐ Very Good   ☐ Good   ☐ Fair   ☐ Poor   ☐ Unable to rate

Comments _____

_____

Collections

☐ Excellent   ☐ Very Good   ☐ Good   ☐ Fair   ☐ Poor   ☐ Unable to rate

Comments _____

_____

Staff

☐ Excellent   ☐ Very Good   ☐ Good   ☐ Fair   ☐ Poor   ☐ Unable to rate

Comments _____

_____

Hours

☐ Excellent   ☐ Very Good   ☐ Good   ☐ Fair   ☐ Poor   ☐ Unable to rate

Comments _____

_____

Facilities (temperature, lighting, study space, etc.)

☐ Excellent   ☐ Very Good   ☐ Good   ☐ Fair   ☐ Poor   ☐ Unable to rate

Comments _____

_____

2. How frequently do you use Schmidt Library?

☐ Never   ☐ Once a year   ☐ Once a semester   ☐ Once a month   ☐ Twice a month

☐ Once a week   ☐ Twice a week   ☐ More often

Why do you use the Library? (Check all that apply.)

☐ Class assignments   ☐ Place material on reserve

☐ Research   ☐ Class preparation

☐ Recreational reading   ☐ Other

☐ AV   Please describe _____

_____

3. Please place a **single** checkmark by the services you have used and **two** checkmarks by   those you use regularly:

☐ Schmidt Library Web   ☐ Reference materials

☐ Books   ☐ Reference librarians/research assistance

☐ Periodicals   ☐ Classroom instruction

☐ AV equipment   ☐ Photocopy machines

☐ AV collection   ☐ Interlibrary loan

☐ Reserves   ☐ Conference Rooms

☐ Archives, Special Collections   ☐ Study areas

4. Background Information

☐ Full-time faculty

☐ Part-time faculty

Department _____   **Sex**   ☐ Male   ☐ Female

Length of service at YCP

☐ 1-5years   ☐ 6-10 years   ☐ 11-15 years   ☐ 16-20 years   ☐ 21-24 years   ☐ 25+ years

Do you ever use the Schmidt Library Web from your home?   ☐ Yes   ☐ No

Please note any additional comments which would assist us in planning for Schmidt Library in the 2002-2007 long range planning cycle.

DOCUMENTS

STUDENT SURVEYS

PORTER HENDERSON LIBRARY
STUDENT SURVEY
Spring 2006

1. What is your present classification?

    ☐Freshman   ☐Sophomore   ☐Junior   ☐Senior   ☐Graduate Student

2. In which of the following colleges is your major?

    ☐Business ☐Education ☐Liberal and Fine Arts ☐Sciences ☐Undeclared

    _____Major

3. Your Age.

    ☐ 22 or younger   ☐23-25   ☐26-35   ☐36-45   ☐46+

4. Please indicate how satisfied you are with the following Library services and resources.
    (USE THE FOLLOWING SCALE FOR EACH ITEM LISTED: 5=VERY SATISFIED, 4=SOMEWHAT SATISFIED, 3=NEUTRAL, 2=SOMEWHAT DISSATISFIED, 1=VERY DISSATISFIED, X=NEVER USED.)

    Online databases___   Online catalog (RamCat)___   Reference Services___

    Circulation Services___   Media Services___   Course Reserves Services___

    Interlibrary Loan___   Library Tab on RamPort____

    Weekday hours ____   Weekend hours____   Summer hours___

Current Library Hours	Fall and Spring	Summer
M-Th	7:30am to 2am	7:30am to 11pm
F	7:30am to 6pm	7:30am to 6pm
Sa	9am to 6pm	9am to 6pm
Su	1pm to midnight	1pm to 11pm

Comments:_____

_____

_____

(FOR QUESTION 5, PLEASE USE A SCALE OF 5=ONCE A WEEK OR MORE, 4=ONCE EVERY TWO OR THREE WEEKS, 3=ONCE A MONTH, 2=ONCE OR TWICE A SEMSTER, 1=NEVER.)

5. How often do you need to seek assistance with your class assignments and research from

Librarians___   Instructors___   Other students___   Others___ : Please specify_____

[Please turn over and complete page 2.]

For questions 6 to 12 indicate the extent to which you agree or disagree with the following statements. **(USE THE FOLLOWING SCALE AND CIRCLE ONE RESPONSE FOR EACH STATEMENT: 5=STRONGLY AGREE, 4=AGREE, 3=NEUTRAL, 2=DISAGREE, 1=STRONGLY DISAGREE, X=DON'T KNOW.)**

6.   The Library has the online resources I need to complete my research.

     5   4   3   2   1   X

7.   The Library provides access to the information I need for class assignments.

     5   4   3   2   1   X

8.   The Reference Desk staff members provide knowledgeable assistance for your information needs.

     5   4   3   2   1   X

9.   The Reference Desk staff members provide friendly service.

     5   4   3   2   1   X

10.   The Library's web pages are helpful.

     5   4   3   2   1   X

11.   The Library Tab on RamPort is helpful.

     5   4   3   2   1   X

12.   Classes with library instruction and/or that use one of the Library's online tutorials are helpful.

     5   4   3   2   1   X

Comments for Questions 6-12:_____

_____

_____

What specific improvements would you suggest for the Library's information services and resources?

_____

_____

_____

_____

Columbia Union College

Weis Library Survey - Spring 2006

Please help us evaluate Weis Library's services and resources by filling out this brief survey. Fill in the appropriate circles using a dark pencil or pen. If you have already filled out the survey in another class this spring, please do not do so again. Thank you.

Class Standing: Major:_____

      Freshman

      Sophomore

      Junior

      Senior

      Other

Program:

      Traditional

      Adult Evening Program - Takoma Park

      Adult Evening Program - Gaithersburg

1. How often have your class assignments required you to use library resources this semester?

      Frequently

      Occasionally

      Never

2. Were you satisfied with the service you received from the Weis Library staff?

      Yes

      No

  If not, how could the service have been improved? _____

_____

3. Has Weis Library had the resources needed for your courses at CUC?

      Yes

      No

  If not, for what were you looking? _____

4. If you used Weis Library's electronic resources, where were you usually?

      In the library

      In your dormitory room

      In an on-campus computer lab

      Off campus   Please turn page over

5. How often did you use CUC departmental libraries (e.g., Business Dept., Math, Music, Nursing, Religion)?

        Frequently

        Occasionally

        Never

6. If you used libraries other than the Weis Library, why did you do so? _____

_____

_____

7. Have you used the following Weis Library resources and services?   Fill in Yes or No for each item

    <u>Yes</u>   <u>No</u>

                      Computers for Internet research

                      Computers for periodical indexes and other databases

                      Magazines

                      Newspapers

                      Materials placed on reserve by your instructors

                      Reference books

                      Books checked out (other than reserve books)

                      Interlibrary loan service (requested via paper form)

                      Consortium loans (requested electronically and delivered by courier)

                      Individual study

                      Group study

                      Curriculum Library

                      Consultation with librarians

                      Copy machine

                      Other:_____

8. The college is planning to build a new building which will include a new library. What would you like to see in the new library?

Comments (optional):

Jamestown College

Raugust Library
Library Satisfaction Questionnaire
April, 2005

The library staff is constantly trying to improve library services for the students and faculty. Thank you for helping us in this effort by completing this questionnaire.

Class this semester: _____ Freshman _____ Sophomore _____ Junior
_____ Senior _____ Other

What is your major? (optional) _____
no major _____

1. **How often to you come to the library?**

    _____ Daily
    _____ Several times a week
    _____ Once a week
    _____ Once a month
    _____ Once a semester
    _____ Never

2. **Why do you come to the library? Check all that apply.**

    _____ Research
    _____ Check out materials from the collection
    _____ Return materials
    _____ Check out a reserve item
    _____ Watch a video
    _____ Listen to a cassette, record, or cd
    _____ Attend a library instruction class
    _____ Use a public computer workstation
    _____ Photocopy
    _____ Study
    _____ Group meeting
    _____ Request or pick up an interlibrary loan item
    _____ Check out av equipment

3. **Were you greeted promptly and courteously at the circulation desk?**

    _____ yes
    _____ no

4. **How satisfied are you with the help you receive, on average, at the circulation desk?**

   Most satisfied   Least satisfied

   ___ 5   ___ 4   ___ 3   ___ 2   ___ 1

5. **Are the checkout periods for materials adequate?**

   _____ yes
   _____ no

6. **Have you ever used ODIN, the online catalog?**

   _____ yes
   _____ no

7. **Did you find it fairly easy to use?**

   _____ yes
   _____ no   Describe any problem:

8. **In general, are you able to find the book or other material on the shelf, once you have identified what you need?**

   _____ yes
   _____ no

9. **How satisfied are you with the *number* of public access terminals in the library?**

   Most satisfied   Least satisfied

   ___ 5   ___ 4   ___ 3   ___ 2   ___ 1

10. **How satisfied are you with the *quality* of the public access terminals in the library?**

    Most satisfied   Least satisfied

    ___ 5   ___ 4   ___ 3   ___ 2   ___ 1

11. **Have you accessed the library homepage from another site on campus?**

_____ yes
_____ no

12. **Have you accessed the library homepage from off campus?**

_____ yes
_____ no

13. **If yes to question 12, did you have any problems with access?**

_____ yes **Describe:**
_____ no

14. **Are you aware of the link from the library homepage to an online resources page for your major?**

_____ yes
_____ no

15. **Check off all the services which you have used from the library's homepage.**

_____ LaND (Library Access North Dakota)
_____ netLibrary
_____ JSTOR
_____ Academic Search Premier
_____ Business Source Premier
_____ CINAHL
_____ CIOS
_____ Classical Music Library
_____ Contemporary Authors
_____ Encyclopedia Britannica
_____ ERIC
_____ ERIC Document Service
_____ FirstSearch
_____ GPO Access
_____ Health Source: Nursing/Academic Edition
_____ Literature Online (LION)
_____ MasterFILE Premier
_____ Medline
_____ National Newspapers
_____ North Dakota Statistical Abstract
_____ OCLC World Cat
_____ Oxford English Dictionary (OED)
_____ Pre-CINAHL

_____ ProQuest Education Journals
_____ ProQuest Psychology Journals
_____ PsychInfo
_____ Regional Business News

16. How satisfied are you with the SCOPE AND VARIETY of these online resources?

Most satisfied   Least satisfied

___ 5   ___ 4   ___ 3   ___ 2   ___ 1

17. What other online resources would you like to add to the library's collection?

18. Have you ever read an ebook from netLibrary?
_____ yes
_____ no

19. If yes, how easy did you find netLibrary to use?

Most difficult   Least difficult

___ 5   ___ 4   ___ 3   ___ 2   ___ 1

20. Have you ever downloaded or printed a full-text article from JSTOR or any other full-text database?

_____ yes
_____ no

21. If yes, how easy did you find the process of downloading or printing?

Most difficult   Least difficult

___ 5   ___ 4   ___ 3   ___ 2   ___ 1

22. How satisfied are you with the BOOK collection in your major?

Most satisfied   Least satisfied

___ 5   ___ 4   ___ 3   ___ 2   ___ 1

23. How satisfied are you with the JOURNAL collection in your major?

Most satisfied   Least satisfied

___ 5   ___ 4   ___ 3   ___ 2   ___ 1

24. How satisfied are you with the AV collection in your major?

Most satisfied   Least satisfied

___ 5   ___ 4   ___ 3   ___ 2   ___ 1

25. How satisfied are you with the library's hours?

Most satisfied   Least satisfied

___ 5   ___ 4   ___ 3   ___ 2   ___ 1

26. If dissatisfied with the library's hours, how would you change them?

27. Have you used interlibrary loan at Raugust Library?

_____ yes
_____ no

28. If yes, how satisfied are you with this service?

Most satisfied   Least satisfied

___ 5   ___ 4   ___ 3   ___ 2   ___ 1

29. If yes, how long did it take (on average) for you to receive your loans?

_____ hours
_____ 1 day
_____ 2 days
_____ 3 days
_____ 1 week
_____ 2 weeks
_____ never

30. Have you ever used the Ariel service for interlibrary loans?
_____ yes
_____ no
_____ not sure

31. If yes, how satisfied are you with this service?

Most satisfied   Least satisfied

__ 5   __ 4   __ 3   __ 2   __ 1

32. Have you ever initiated an electronic interlibrary loan request from an online library resource?

_____ yes
_____ no

33. If yes, how easy did you find it initiate the request?

Most difficult   Least difficult

__ 5   __ 4   __ 3   __ 2   __ 1

34. Have you ever consulted a reference librarian at Raugust Library?

_____ yes
_____ no

35. If yes, how satisfied are you with this service?

Most satisfied   Least satisfied

__ 5   __ 4   __ 3   __ 2   __ 1

36. Have you ever received a class in library use or other instruction from a librarian at Raugust Library?

_____ yes
_____ no

37. If yes, how satisfied are you with this instruction?

Most satisfied   Least satisfied

__ 5   __ 4   __ 3   __ 2   __ 1

38. **Did the instruction occur in the library or in your classroom during a class period?**

_____ library
_____ classroom

39. **Please check off all areas which you would like to have offered as an 8-week class:**

_____ library instruction/orientation
_____ locating and evaluating online resources (information literacy)
_____ specific, targeted instruction in the resources of your major
_____ research methods for Honors Project/Senior Seminar/Masters Thesis
_____ other _____

40. **How comfortable do you find the library on average?**

Most comfortable   Least comfortable

___ 5   ___ 4   ___ 3   ___ 2   ___ 1

41. **How would you change the library's furniture or arrangement?**

42. **Are you aware of the Curriculum Library (children's book collection)?**
_____ yes
_____ no

43. **Are you aware that the library has an elevator?**
_____ yes
_____ no

44. **Other comments:**

Thank you for your time and input!

Spring 2002 Student Survey
Mary Washington College, Simpson Library
Fredericksburg, Virginia

1.1 When you need information about something, where do you go first?

1.1.1   If the Web, what search engine or sites do you use most often?

1.1.2   If Library, what library?

1.1.3   If Library's Web site, what section or area?

1.2 How about when you have a class assignment?

1.2.1   If Web, what search engines or sites do you use most often?

1.2.2   If Library, what library?

1.2.3   If Library's Web site, what section or area?

2.1 Have you ever had a class on doing library research during a course you've taken?

2.1.1   If yes, what departments/subject areas?

2.1.1.1 Did the class(es) help you in your research?

2.1.1.2 Did you ask the librarian for follow-up help?

2.1.2   If no, is it because you haven't had any assignments requiring research?

3.1 Have you found the library's print and electronic resources adequate for your research needs?

3.2 Are the resources easy to find and use?

4.1 Do you prefer printed or online resources?

5.1 You need a book that the library doesn't own. What would do to get it?"

5.2 You need an article from a magazine or journal that the library doesn't own. What would you do to get it?

O'GRADY LIBRARY
SAINT MARTIN'S COLLEGE

Student Survey: Fall 2004

Class and major

Class (circle one):   Freshman   Sophomore   Junior   Senior

                    Graduate student   English as a Second Language   Other

Location (circle one):   Main campus   Fort Lewis extension   McChord extension   Olympic College extension   Other

Major: _____

Do you live (circle one):   On campus   Off campus

Are you (circle one):   Female   Male

Library use--the basics

1)   Have you used the O'Grady Library's services or collections—whether in person, on the Web, or by phone—during the past twelve months?

           Yes   No

2)   If you answered *no* to question # 1, please check the reasons why you *did not* use the library. You then do not need to complete the rest of the survey.

☐   I use the McChord library.

☐   I use other libraries.

☐   I use only resources available on the Internet.

☐   I find the library difficult to use.

☐   I don't get the assistance I need.

☐   My assignments do not require the use of the library.

☐   Other (please explain):

_____

_____

_____

_____

O'Grady Library, Saint Martin's College   Student Survey: Fall 2004

Library use--the details

3) On average, how often do you use the O'Grady Library? Please mark the frequency for each type of use.

	Daily	Weekly	Monthly	Seldom	Never
Visit library in person	☐	☐	☐	☐	☐
Use campus/dorm computer to find library resources	☐	☐	☐	☐	☐
Use off-campus computer to find library resources	☐	☐	☐	☐	☐
Call library by phone	☐	☐	☐	☐	☐

4) Why do you visit the library in person? Mark how often you use the library for each of the activities listed below.

	Daily	Weekly	Monthly	Seldom	Never
Look for journal/newspaper article	☐	☐	☐	☐	☐
Look for book	☐	☐	☐	☐	☐
Watch videos/DVDs	☐	☐	☐	☐	☐
Use a library computer	☐	☐	☐	☐	☐
Course reserves/assigned reading	☐	☐	☐	☐	☐
Interlibrary loan (ILLiad)	☐	☐	☐	☐	☐
Group study	☐	☐	☐	☐	☐
Study alone	☐	☐	☐	☐	☐
Use photocopier	☐	☐	☐	☐	☐
Ask librarian for research assistance	☐	☐	☐	☐	☐
Socialize	☐	☐	☐	☐	☐
Casual reading	☐	☐	☐	☐	☐
Attend class	☐	☐	☐	☐	☐
Ask for technology/computer assistance	☐	☐	☐	☐	☐
Use audiovisual equipment	☐	☐	☐	☐	☐
Use your laptop	☐	☐	☐	☐	☐

5) If you come to the library to use a computer, what do you use it for?

	Daily	Weekly	Monthly	Seldom	Never
Read or send email	☐	☐	☐	☐	☐
Search the library's online catalog	☐	☐	☐	☐	☐
Search an online journal database	☐	☐	☐	☐	☐
Write a research paper	☐	☐	☐	☐	☐
Do research on the Web	☐	☐	☐	☐	☐
Surf the Web	☐	☐	☐	☐	☐
Interlibrary loan (ILLiad)	☐	☐	☐	☐	☐
Use specific software applications for class projects/assignments	☐	☐	☐	☐	☐

6) How often do you use the following software applications on computers in the library?

	Daily	Weekly	Monthly	Seldom	Never
Adobe Photoshop, Acrobat, or other Adobe graphics software	☐	☐	☐	☐	☐
Caere OmniPage or OmniForm	☐	☐	☐	☐	☐
Grade Machine	☐	☐	☐	☐	☐
Inspiration	☐	☐	☐	☐	☐
JAWS, Dragon Naturally Speaking, OpenBook, or MAGic	☐	☐	☐	☐	☐
LOGOS biblical software	☐	☐	☐	☐	☐
Macromedia Dreamweaver, Fireworks, or Flash	☐	☐	☐	☐	☐
MATLAB	☐	☐	☐	☐	☐
Microsoft Office (Word, Excel, PowerPoint, Access, Publisher)	☐	☐	☐	☐	☐
Microsoft FrontPage	☐	☐	☐	☐	☐
Microsoft MovieMaker	☐	☐	☐	☐	☐
Microsoft Project	☐	☐	☐	☐	☐
MINITAB	☐	☐	☐	☐	☐

6) How often do you use the following software applications on computers in the library? *(continued)*

	Daily	Weekly	Monthly	Seldom	Never
NVIVO	[]	[]	[]	[]	[]
Pinnacle	[]	[]	[]	[]	[]
Sound Forge Studio	[]	[]	[]	[]	[]
Vis-à-vis, Nakama, or other foreign language software	[]	[]	[]	[]	[]
Other (please list below)	[]	[]	[]	[]	[]

_____

_____

_____

7) Within the last twelve months, were the following technologies available in the library **when you needed them?**

	Always	Most of the time	Half the time	Seldom	Never	Never used
Computer in Information Commons or downstairs	[]	[]	[]	[]	[]	[]
Laptop	[]	[]	[]	[]	[]	[]
Network connection for laptop	[]	[]	[]	[]	[]	[]
Scanner	[]	[]	[]	[]	[]	[]
Digital camera	[]	[]	[]	[]	[]	[]
Digital video camera	[]	[]	[]	[]	[]	[]
Video camera (VHS)	[]	[]	[]	[]	[]	[]
Video editing technologies (e.g., Pinnacle or FireWire)	[]	[]	[]	[]	[]	[]
Graphics editing technologies	[]	[]	[]	[]	[]	[]
TV with VCR/DVD	[]	[]	[]	[]	[]	[]
Audio equipment (e.g., stereo or cassette recorder)	[]	[]	[]	[]	[]	[]

7) Within the last twelve months, were the following technologies available in the library **when you needed them?** *(continued)*

	Always	Most of the time	Half the time	Seldom	Never	Never used
Computer with course-specific software	☐	☐	☐	☐	☐	☐
Other (please list below):	☐	☐	☐	☐	☐	☐

_____

_____

_____

Library satisfaction

8) How satisfied are you with the library's collections and other resources?

	Very satisfied	Satisfied	Neutral	Dissatisfied	Very Dissatisfied	Never used
Books	☐	☐	☐	☐	☐	☐
Print journals and newspapers	☐	☐	☐	☐	☐	☐
Microform journals and newspapers	☐	☐	☐	☐	☐	☐
Electronic full-text journals	☐	☐	☐	☐	☐	☐
Electronic books	☐	☐	☐	☐	☐	☐
Online databases	☐	☐	☐	☐	☐	☐
Reference books (main level)	☐	☐	☐	☐	☐	☐
Audiovisual items (videos, CDs, DVDs, etc.)	☐	☐	☐	☐	☐	☐
Curriculum collection	☐	☐	☐	☐	☐	☐
Course reserves	☐	☐	☐	☐	☐	☐
Computer equipment	☐	☐	☐	☐	☐	☐

8)　How satisfied are you with the library's collections and other resources?　(*continued*)

	Very satisfied	Satisfied	Neutral	Dissatisfied	Very Dissatisfied	Never used
Software applications	[]	[]	[]	[]	[]	[]
Audiovisual equipment (cameras, VCRs, etc.)	[]	[]	[]	[]	[]	[]
Library technology classrooms	[]	[]	[]	[]	[]	[]

9)　How satisfied are you with the library's services?

	Very satisfied	Satisfied	Neutral	Dissatisfied	Very Dissatisfied	Never used
Availability of computer assistance when you need it	[]	[]	[]	[]	[]	[]
Availability of research assistance when you need it	[]	[]	[]	[]	[]	[]
Helpfulness of reference desk staff	[]	[]	[]	[]	[]	[]
Helpfulness of circulation desk staff	[]	[]	[]	[]	[]	[]
Interlibrary loan (ILLiad)	[]	[]	[]	[]	[]	[]
Loan periods for library materials	[]	[]	[]	[]	[]	[]
Library research instruction or training	[]	[]	[]	[]	[]	[]
Library Web site	[]	[]	[]	[]	[]	[]
Technology instruction or training	[]	[]	[]	[]	[]	[]

Saint Martin's University

10) In the past year, did the library have all of the software you needed to accomplish your academic work? (If *no*, please list software needed.)

Yes   No

_____

_____

_____

11) In the past year, did the library have all of the computing and audiovisual equipment you needed to accomplish your academic work? (If *no*, please list software needed.)

Yes   No

_____

_____

_____

12) How satisfied are you with the library overall?

Very satisfied	Satisfied	Neutral	Dissatisfied	Very Dissatisfied	Never used
☐	☐	☐	☐	☐	☐

13) If you want to elaborate on any of the questions above or if there are areas of concern or interest which were not addressed in the survey, please use this space. In particular, are there additional services or materials that you feel the O'Grady Library should provide or improve?

_____

_____

_____

_____

_____

_____

_____

_____

_____

_____

MILLER F. WHITTAKER LIBRARY
GRADUATE/DOCTORAL
USER SURVEY

> The Miller F. Whittaker Library staff is conducting a survey to determine library use. Please take a few minutes to answer the following questions. Thank you for your cooperation and participation.

April 2004

1. What is your academic classification?

   ( ) Masters   ( ) Specialist   ( ) Doctorate

2. How often do you **come to the library**?

   ( ) Daily   ( ) Weekly   ( ) Monthly   ( ) Once a semester or less   ( ) Never

3. How often do you **use the library's web site**?

   ( ) Daily   ( ) Weekly   ( ) Monthly   ( ) Once a semester or less   ( ) Never

4. What day(s) of the week do you come to the library most?

   ( ) Monday   ( ) Tuesday   ( ) Wednesday   ( ) Thursday   ( ) Friday   ( ) Saturday   ( ) Sunday

5. Are there times when you would like to use the facilities or services when they are not available?

   ( ) yes   ( ) no

   If yes, *please explain*

6. What source(s), other than Miller F. Whittaker Library, do you use to obtain information?
   (*Mark all that apply*)

   ( ) Departmental resources in my discipline   ( ) A non-SCSU academic library

   ( ) A public library   ( ) A special library   ( ) SCSU library's website

   ( ) Other *Specify*_____

7. Are you satisfied with the library's current Saturday hours?
   Sat. 11:00-6:00p.m.

   ( ) yes   ( ) no

   If not, please select one of the following options for Saturday hours:

   ( ) Sat. 10:00-5:00 p.m.

   ( ) Sat. 9:00-4:00 p.m.

   ( ) Other (*Specify*) _____

St. John Fisher College
Lavery Library Focus Group
STUDENT QUESTIONS

1. **What are three things you like about the library?**

   What are three things you'd like to see improved at the library?

2. **What do you like about the library website?**

   What improvements need to be made to the website?

3. **How could the technology at the library be improved to help you work more efficiently? (computers, printers, microfiche, etc.)**

4. **What are some problems you have encountered when obtaining information resources for your coursework?**

   How could the library alleviate these problems?

5. **What are your expectations of the library staff? How can the staff help with your library needs?**

   Reference librarians:
   Support staff:
   Work-study students:

   How is their friendliness? Effort? Attitude?

   Reference librarians:
   Support staff:
   Work-study students:

6. **Please rank-order the best way for you to learn how to use the library's resources and all it has to offer?**

   Other ways to learn how to use the library and all it has to offer:

7. **Do you have any recommendations, other than those already mentioned, for future improvements in the library?**

Schmidt Library
Student Use Survey   **Spring 2006**

We are assessing user satisfaction with collections, services, facilities, staff, and hours. So we can better serve your needs, please take a few minutes to answer these questions. Please return the survey to Raeann Waltersdorf via campus mail or drop your questionnaire at Information Services by **March 22, 2006**. Thank you.

1. In evaluating Schmidt Library, how would you rate our

Services

☐ Excellent   ☐ Very Good   ☐ Good   ☐ Fair   ☐ Poor   ☐ Unable to rate

Comments _____

_____

Schmidt Library Web/Online Systems

☐ Excellent   ☐ Very Good   ☐ Good   ☐ Fair   ☐ Poor   ☐ Unable to rate

Comments _____

_____

Collections

☐ Excellent   ☐ Very Good   ☐ Good   ☐ Fair   ☐ Poor   ☐ Unable to rate

Comments _____

_____

Staff

☐ Excellent   ☐ Very Good   ☐ Good   ☐ Fair   ☐ Poor   ☐ Unable to rate

Comments _____

_____

Hours

☐ Excellent   ☐ Very Good   ☐ Good   ☐ Fair   ☐ Poor   ☐ Unable to rate

Comments _____

_____

Facilities (temperature, lighting, study space, etc.)

☐ Excellent   ☐ Very Good   ☐ Good   ☐ Fair   ☐ Poor   ☐ Unable to rate

Comments _____

_____

2. After the renovation and reorganization of services, how would you rate our (Mark N/A if you were not here before the 2004 renovation and reorganization.)

Services

☐ Better ☐ No Change ☐ Worse ☐ N/A

Comments _____

_____

Schmidt Library Web/Online Systems

☐ Better ☐ No Change ☐ Worse ☐ N/A

Comments _____

_____

Collections (books, periodicals, media, online)

☐ Better ☐ No Change ☐ Worse ☐ N/A

Comments _____

_____

Staff

☐ Better ☐ No Change ☐ Worse ☐ N/A

Comments _____

_____

Hours

☐ Better ☐ No Change ☐ Worse ☐ N/A

Comments _____

_____

Facilities (temperature, lighting, study space, etc.)

☐ Better ☐ No Change ☐ Worse ☐ N/A

Comments _____

_____

3. How frequently do you use Schmidt Library?

☐ Never ☐ Once a year ☐ Once a semester ☐ Once a month ☐ Twice a month

☐ Once a week ☐ Twice a week ☐ More often

4. Why do you use the Library? (Check all that apply.)

☐ Research   ☐ Class preparation   ☐ Wireless network

☐ Recreational reading/media   ☐ Study/work   ☐ Group study rooms

☐ Instructional media (AV)   ☐ Socializing   ☐ PC workstations

☐ Reserves   ☐ Photocopying   ☐ Don't use

☐ Document Delivery (Interlibrary loan)   ☐ Other (please describe)_____

5. Indicate how often you use the following services.

	Use regularly	Use infrequently	Never Use
Schmidt Library Web	☐	☐	☐
Books	☐	☐	☐
Periodicals	☐	☐	☐
Instructional Media Equipment	☐	☐	☐
Instructional Media Collection	☐	☐	☐
Reserves	☐	☐	☐
Archives, Special Collections	☐	☐	☐
Reference materials (encyclopedias, dictionaries)	☐	☐	☐
Research librarians/research assistance	☐	☐	☐
Photocopy machines	☐	☐	☐
Document Delivery (Interlibrary loan)	☐	☐	☐
Conference rooms	☐	☐	☐
Study areas	☐	☐	☐
PC Workstations	☐	☐	☐
Wireless network	☐	☐	☐
Group study rooms	☐	☐	☐

6. Do you use Schmidt Library Web resources: (Check all that apply.)

☐ in the library

☐ from dormitory

☐ from IT labs

☐ from home

☐ from work

7. What types of virtual resources do you use: (Check all that apply.)

☐ Online books

☐ Online reference sources (encyclopedias, directories, dictionaries, citation manuals, etc.)

☐ Online journal articles

☐ Online newspaper articles

8. Please note ways we can improve which would assist us in planning for Schmidt Library in the 2007-2012 long range planning cycle.

Services

Schmidt Library Web/online systems

Collections

Staff

Hours

Facilities

9. Please note any additional comments which would assist us In planning for Schmidt Library in the next YCP long range planning cycle.

10. Background Information

Class

☐ Freshman   ☐ Sophomore   ☐ Junior   ☐ Senior

☐ Business masters' program   ☐ Nursing masters' program   ☐ Education masters' program

Sex   ☐ Male   ☐ Female   **Age** _____

Major _____   **Status**   ☐ Full-time   ☐ Part-time   ☐ Non-credit

Residence   **Do you ever use Schmidt Library Web from your residence?**

☐ On campus   ☐ Off campus   ☐ Yes   ☐ No

Documents: Student Surveys - 90

DOCUMENTS

GENERAL SURVEYS

Ross Pendergraft Library & Technology Center
Arkansas Tech University

User Survey

What is your classification or status at the university?
Undergraduate Student
Graduate Student
Faculty
Staff
Administration

What school, program, or administrative area are you affiliated with?
School of Business
School of Education
School of Community Education and Development
School of Liberal & Fine Arts
School of Physical & Life Sciences
School of Systems Science
Graduate Studies
Academic Affairs
Administration & Finance
Development
Student Services

How often do you come into the library?
Daily
Several times a week
Once a week
Several times a month
Rarely

How often do you access library web pages from outside the library building?
Daily
Several times a week
Once a week
Several times a month
Rarely or not at all

How satisfied are you with library services?
Very Satisfied
Satisfied
Somewhat Satisfied
Unsatisfied
Very Unsatisfied

Which of the following library resources & services have you used this year? (Please select all that apply.)
Books
Periodicals (journals, newspapers, or magazines in print or microform)
Media (audio or video materials in a variety of formats)
Library website
Library online catalog

Golden Library User Survey - 2005

We are asking for your help in identifying levels and patterns of use, levels of satisfaction, and user-based priorities for Golden Library. We want to know how we can better serve the ENMU community.

1. Purpose for visit. (Check all that apply.)

☐ a. Instructor assigned specific library work.
☐ b. Came to study.
☐ c. Research for assigned paper.
☐ d. Personal research.
☐ e. Leisure time (chat, email, internet).
☐ f. Media Resources.

☐ g. Look at art work.
☐ h. Meet others/study group.
☐ i. Check out/renew books.
☐ j. Make copies.
☐ k. Computer Lab.
☐ j. Other_____

2. With this visit,

☐ a. I accomplished everything I wanted.
☐ b. I accomplished almost everything I wanted.
☐ c. I accomplished almost none of my goals because:

_____
_____

4. Did you ask for help

☐ a. from a reference librarian?
☐ b. from a library staff member?
☐ c. from a student worker in the library?
☐ d. from a fellow student?
☐ e. No.

5. Estimate how often you visit the library each semester.

☐ a. 1-2 times
☐ b. 3-5 times
☐ c. 6-10 times
☐ d. more than 10 times

6. What is your major/discipline? _____

7. If you received library instruction, how useful was it? Answer all that apply and rate according to the usefulness of the instruction.

	Useful	Somewhat useful	Not useful
a. Printed guides	☐	☐	☐
b. Face to face at Reference Desk	☐	☐	☐
c. Freshman Seminar tours	☐	☐	☐
d. Instruction as part of class	☐	☐	☐
e. Other_____	☐	☐	☐

8. Your ENMU status

☐ a. Undergraduate   ☐ c. Faculty   ☐ e. Community Member
☐ b. Graduate   ☐ d. Staff   ☐ f. Other_____

9. How well satisfied are you with the physical facilities of the library?

☐ a. Very satisfied   ☐ c. Somewhat satisfied
☐ b. Satisfied   ☐ d. Unsatisfied   Please Turn Over →

10. How satisfied are you overall with the quality of library services?
    ☐a. Very satisfied   ☐c. Somewhat satisfied
    ☐b. Satisfied   ☐d. Unsatisfied

11. How satisfied are you overall with library collections?

	Very Satisfied	Satisfied	Somewhat Satisfied	Unsatisfied	N/A
a. Print journals/newspapers	☐	☐	☐	☐	☐
b. Video/CDs	☐	☐	☐	☐	☐
c. Online Databases & Journals	☐	☐	☐	☐	☐
d. Reference Materials	☐	☐	☐	☐	☐
e. Books	☐	☐	☐	☐	☐
f. Government Documents	☐	☐	☐	☐	☐
g. IRC/Juvenile	☐	☐	☐	☐	☐
h. Special Collections	☐	☐	☐	☐	☐

12. When you have completed your research topic, which of the following are you likely to have used? Check all that apply.
    ☐a. Reference librarian
    ☐b. Electronic databases
    ☐c. LIBROS, the online catalog
    ☐d. Shelf browsing
    ☐e. Internet surfing

13. When the library lacks the materials you need, what do you do?
    ☐a. Request Interlibrary Loan.
    ☐b. Check other local libraries.
    ☐c. Use the Internet.
    ☐d. Get a "passport" to other academic libraries in NM & TX.
    ☐e. Change topics.
    ☐f. Other_____

14. Which of the library's web pages have you used? Check all that apply.
    ☐Library Catalog   ☐Library Departments
    ☐Databases & Journals   ☐Library Map/Virtual tour
    ☐Interlibrary Loan   ☐Library Information

15. How would you rate the use of Library's web pages?
    ☐a. Excellent   ☐c. Average
    ☐b. Good   ☐d. Hard

16. What new services or building changes should the library implement?
_____
_____
_____

17. How might the library better serve your needs?_____
_____
_____
_____
_____

Elon University

PLEASE HELP US WITH THIS BRIEF SURVEY!

Which library services are important to you? Please mark each item on the scale of 1 to 5, with 1 being "not important at all" and 5 being "extremely important."

1=not important -- 5=extremely important

Knowledgeable library staff are available to help you	1	2	3	4	5
Library owns the books and journals I need	1	2	3	4	5
Books and journals are shelved correctly	1	2	3	4	5
Library owns a broad range of online resources	1	2	3	4	5
Library web page is easy to use	1	2	3	4	5
Library catalog is accurate and easy to use	1	2	3	4	5
Library orientation and research classes are available	1	2	3	4	5
Interlibrary loan is fast and effective	1	2	3	4	5
Photocopiers are working	1	2	3	4	5
Computers and printers are working	1	2	3	4	5
Library is a quiet and comfortable place to study	1	2	3	4	5
Library has an adequate number of group study rooms	1	2	3	4	5
I can bring food and drink into the library	1	2	3	4	5
Course material is available on reserves	1	2	3	4	5
Writing and Tutoring Centers are in the library	1	2	3	4	5
Media Services are in the library	1	2	3	4	5
Academic Computing services are in the library	1	2	3	4	5
The library is open late at night	1	2	3	4	5
The library is open on weekends	1	2	3	4	5

What is your University status? __Undergraduate student __Graduate student __ Faculty __Staff __ Other

How often do you come to the library? __Once a semester __Once a month __2/3 times a month __Once a week __Several times a week __Every day

IF YOU HAVE TIME, PLEASE ANSWER THE QUESTIONS ON THE REVERSE SIDE.

THANK YOU FOR YOUR HELP!

Elon University

Thank you for your comments!

1. What library services are most important to you? What would you hate to see us change?

2. What library services would you like us to improve, or to add?

BELK LIBRARY

2550 CAMPUS BOX

Library Survey

Our library staff needs your cooperation in obtaining information concerning the daily use made of the library. Your answers will assist us in enhancing library services. Please take a moment and answer the questions below. Thank you for your cooperation!

1. My status is:
   - ○ Student
   - ○ Faculty/Staff
   - ○ Other

2. My reason(s) for coming to the Library is: (Check all that apply)
   - ☐ Check-Out/Return/Renew Books
   - ☐ Use Reserve Materials
   - ☐ Research
   - ☐ Study
   - ☐ Check Email
   - ☐ Use Computer Lab
   - ☐ Attend a class
   - ☐ Other: (List all other reasons)
   _____
   _____

3. Materials I used while in the Library were:
   - ☐ Books
   - ☐ Government Documents
   - ☐ Journals (microfiche, bound, microfilm)
   - ☐ Newspaper
   - ☐ A-V Materials (videos, CDs, tapes)
   - ☐ Online (e-books, e-journals, e-gov. docs)
   - ☐ Other (music lab, reserves, etc)

4. Did you find the materials you needed?
   - ○ Yes
   - ○ No
   If no, please indicate your research topic:
   _____

5. On the computers I used: (Check all that apply)
   - ☐ GALILEO
   - ☐ GIL
   - ☐ Internet-Course Related
   - ☐ Internet-Personal Use
   - ☐ E-mail
   - ☐ WebCT (online assignments)

6. Did you receive assistance that you required from the Library staff?
   - ○ Yes
   - ○ Somewhat
   - ○ No

7. Please make comments and suggestions below.

DUGGAN LIBRARY SURVEY

For the next two weeks, the Duggan Library will be conducting a survey of your opinions of the library, its services and collection. Please take a few minutes of your time to answer the following questions. When completed, place the survey in boxes marked "Library Survey" in student mailbox area or in the library at the Circulation Desk by March 19. Thank you in advance.

Please let us know who you are: (please circle)

Freshman   Sophomore   Junior   Senior   Faculty/staff   Community patron   Visitor to college

Library Personnel

➢ If you need help in the library, where do you usually go to find it? (please circle)

Circulation Desk   Reference Desk   ask fellow student who's also in the library   other _____

➢ If you need help in the library, whom do you usually ask? (please circle)

person at Circ. Desk   person at Reference Desk   library staff member   library *student* staff member

friend who's also studying at the library   my professor   other _____

➢ Are you generally satisfied with the library assistance you get from this person?   Yes   No

If yes, how was the person helpful to you? _____

If no, how could their assistance be improved? _____

The Library As A Place To Study

➢ Please circle the + that most closely reflects your response to these statements: (agree, no opinion, disagree)

	Agree ---- No op. --- Disagree
The open hours of the library are convenient for me.	+--------------+--------------+
The library environment (acoustics, temperature, lighting) is conducive to studying.	+--------------+--------------+
The library is a quiet place to study.	+--------------+--------------+
Checkout procedures are performed in a timely manner.	+--------------+--------------+
There are enough tables and chairs in the study areas.	+--------------+--------------+
There are enough separate study rooms.	+--------------+--------------+
There are enough public computers available.	+--------------+--------------+
There are enough printers available.	+--------------+--------------+

Comments: _____
_____

-OVER-

Library Resources

Please circle the + that most closely reflects your response to these statements (agree, no opinion, disagree):

Agree --- No op. --- Disagree

➢ Overall, the Duggan Library's collection meets the needs of my assignments.   +---------------+------------+

➢ Specifically, the library has adequate resources in the following areas for my classwork:

Agree --- No op. --- Disagree

- Books   +---------------+------------+
- Periodicals/journals/magazines   +---------------+------------+
- Newspapers   +---------------+------------+
- Government Documents   +---------------+------------+
- Reference Collection (encyclopedias, dictionaries, etc.)   +---------------+------------+

➢ It is easy to find the materials and information I need, such as:

Agree --- No op. --- Disagree

- Books   +---------------+------------+
- Periodicals/journals/magazines   +---------------+------------+
- Newspapers   +---------------+------------+
- Government Documents   +---------------+------------+
- Reference Collection (encyclopedias, dictionaries, etc.)   +---------------+------------+
- Microfilm/microfiche   +---------------+------------+

Agree --- No op. --- Disagree

➢ I am comfortable retrieving and using information electronically   +---------------+------------+

➢ I am comfortable using the library's Web site for accessing information   +---------------+------------+

➢ Printed books and journals will continue to be important sources in the coming years   +---------------+------------+

➢ When I find information online, I print it out to read   +---------------+------------+

➢ The Internet has changed the way I use the library   +---------------+------------+

➢ To find a journal (periodical) citation, I usually use: (please circle):

EBSCOHost   JSTOR   Project MUSE   print indexes   other: _____

➢ Where do you find the majority of your articles?

EBSCOHost   JSTOR   Project MUSE   library stack   interlibrary loan   other_____

➢ In general, using the above sources, have you been able to find the information you need? (please circle)   Yes   N

➢ Have you used Interlibrary Loan to obtain materials not available in the Duggan Library? (please circle)   Yes   N

➢ If so, have you been satisfied with the ILL service? (please circle) Yes No Sometimes

Comments: _____

➢ If no, what problem did you have: (please circle)

Material arrived too late to be useful for the assignment Library was not able to obtain what I needed.

Other: _____

➢ Have you used any of the following resources in the Library: (please circle)

Reserve material kept at the Circulation Desk Archives/Special Collections Videos DVDs Music CDs

➢ Were you satisfied with the information you received from these resources? Yes No

If not, why not? _____

Library Instruction

Have you had a library instruction session by one of the librarians? Yes No

Have you had more than one library instruction session? Yes No

Did the session give you what you needed to use the library? Yes No

Did it skip any information you would like to have had? Yes No

If yes, what information would you like to see included in future sessions? _____
_____

What information from the session was the most useful to you? _____

Library Equipment

➢ Which of these pieces of equipment do you regularly use? (please circle)

photocopier microfilm/microfiche reader/printer Internet terminals

Have you had any problems with any of this equipment? Yes No

If yes, please describe the problem: _____

Do you find the written instructions posted near the equipment to be adequate? Yes No

-OVER-

Your Library Visit

➤ How often do you use the library resources?

Daily   Once a week   Twice a week   Three times a week   Rarely   Never

The questions below pertain to your most recent library visit:

➤ If you were looking for information, what type of information were seeking? _____

_____

➤ Was this for a class or for your own interest and information? (please circle)   Class   Own interest

➤ Were you able to find this information?   Yes   No

➤ What sources did you use to help locate this information? (circle all that apply)

online catalog   online library databases   WWW   personal assistance from library staff member

personal assistance from library student staff member   Reference materials   Print indexes

other: _____

➤ About how long did it take you to find what you were looking for? _____

Suggestions:

The library needs MORE books on: _____

The library needs MORE periodicals on: _____

The library needs MORE electronic resources on: _____

The strongest aspect of the Duggan Library is: _____

The weakest aspect of the Duggan Library is: _____

I have these other suggestions to improve the library: _____

_____

Any other comments? _____

Thank you for taking the time to help us!

This survey is confidential. However, if you would like a response to your comments or concerns, please provide your name and contact information and a librarian will be in touch with you.

Name: _____   *Email:* _____   *Phone number:* _____

Schewe Library Survey

1. My association with Illinois College is...
    ___ First Year   ___ Soph   ___ Junior   ___ Senior
    ___ Staff   ___ Admin   ___ Faculty (non-tenured)   ___ Faculty (tenured)

2. How often have you used the library in person this school year?
    _____ Never
    _____ less than once a month
    _____ about once a month
    _____ about once a week
    _____ 2-3 times per week
    _____ 4 or more times per week

3. Was your last attempt to borrow a book from another library through I-Share (previously called ILCSO) successful?
    _____ Yes   _____ No   _____ Does not apply

4. Mark your top three uses of the library:
    _____ photocopying
    _____ research
    _____ study
    _____ read magazines or newspapers
    _____ email
    _____ class reserves
    _____ meet friends

5. The library collection needs more...
    _____ online databases
    _____ full text databases
    _____ popular music & videos
    _____ popular fiction
    _____ academic non-fiction
    _____ print periodical indexes
    _____ other

    If you selected "other," please briefly describe the need below:

6. Mark the three physical improvements that you consider most important:
    _____ more lighting
    _____ comfortable chairs
    _____ better functioning heating & air conditioning
    _____ more electrical outlets
    _____ less noise
    _____ more group study areas

7. Do you like to study in the library? If not, why?

8. Mark the three service improvements you consider most important:
   _____ expanded weekend hours
   _____ more reliable printers
   _____ more staff scheduled at the circulation desk (instead of the bell)
   _____ color printing
   _____ wireless network
   _____ more staff scheduled at the reference desk
   _____ computer tech support in the library

9. What strengths do you see in the library?
   _____ staff helpfulness
   _____ good collection
   _____ useful databases
   _____ long hours
   _____ other (please explain)

   If you selected "other," please briefly describe the strength below

10. What would make Schewe Library more useful to you?

Tarleton State University

General Satisfaction Survey

PLEASE HELP US IMPROVE LIBRARY SERVICE BY ANSWERING A FEW QUESTIONS.

1) Your campus:

○ Stephenville
○ Killeen
○ Other (please specify)

If you selected other, please specify:

2) Your status:

○ Tarleton Undergraduate
○ Tarleton Graduate Student
○ Faculty
○ Research Staff
○ Staff
○ Other (CTC student, high school student, guest)

3) Your college:

○ Liberal and Fine Arts
○ Education
○ Business Administration
○ Agriculture and Human Sciences
○ Science and Technology
○ Not applicable

4) Are you accessing the library from:

○ Library
○ Office
○ Home
○ Computer Lab
○ Residence Hall
○ Other (please specify)

If you selected other, please specify:

5) What did you do in the library today? How successful were you?

	Did not do	Not successful	Somewhat successful	Neither successful nor unsuccessful	Successful	Very successful
Found a particular item	○	■	○	■	○	■
Researched a topic	○	■	○	■	○	■
Reviewed current literature	○	■	○	■	○	■
Searched the Internet	○	■	○	■	○	■
Checked my email	○	■	○	■	○	■
Used word processor or other Microsoft software	○	■	○	■	○	■
Studied	○	■	○	■	○	■
Used a laptop	○	■	○	■	○	■
Asked a question	○	■	○	■	○	■
Other	○	■	○	■	○	■

6) Overall, how satisfied are you with your library visit today?

○ 1 (Dissatisfied)
○ 2
○ 3
○ 4
○ 5 (Very satisfied)

7) How easy was the library to use today?

○ 1 (Difficult)
○ 2
○ 3
○ 4
○ 5 (Very easy)

8) Today's visit was primarily for:

DOCUMENTS

SPECIAL SERVICES SURVEYS

Elon University

INTERLIBRARY LOAN SURVEY

Please take a moment to answer the questions below, and return this survey by May 1, 2002 to either the Circulation Desk in Belk Library or CB 2550. Your answers will help us improve our services. Thank you very much!

Please check your status:

☐ freshman	☐ graduate student
☐ sophomore	☐ faculty member
☐ junior	☐ Elon staff member
☐ senior	☐ other; please specify: _____

Department/discipline (if applicable, please specify) _____

1. During the 2001/2002 Spring Semester, did you request any materials through Interlibrary Loan?

    ☐ Yes   ☐ No

2. If you rarely or never requested items not owned by Elon University Library, why not? (Please check all that apply.)

    ☐ I'm new to Elon this semester.
    ☐ Found what I needed in Elon's library.
    ☐ Did not need books or articles for my assignments.
    ☐ Went to other libraries/bookstores on my own.
    ☐ The item(s) I needed would not have arrived on time.
    ☐ The item(s) I needed are not available through these services.
    ☐ Did not know I could get items from other libraries.
    ☐ Did not know how to request items, or who to talk to.
    ☐ The request process seemed too complicated.
    ☐ Could not get the help I needed to place a request.
    ☐ Do not know how to find titles of materials that the library does not own.
    ☐ Returning to the library would be too inconvenient.
    ☐ Other _____

_____

** Note - If you have **NOT** requested any interlibrary loan materials, please stop here and return your survey.*
    *If you **HAVE** requested interlibrary loan materials, please continue...*

3. During the 2001/2002 Spring Semester, approximately how many books did you request from other libraries?

    ☐ 1-5 books   ☐ 6-10 books   ☐ more than 10 books   ☐ Other _____

4. During the 2001/2002 Spring Semester, approximately how many photocopies of articles did you request from journals not owned by Elon University Library?

    ☐ 1-5 copies   ☐ 6-10 copies   ☐ more than 10 copies   ☐ Other _____

5. How many items do you usually request at one time?

    ☐ 1-5   ☐ 6-10   ☐ more than 10   ☐ Other _____

-over-

6   After each statement below, please indicate your opinion by circling the appropriate number:

(1) strongly agree   (2) agree   (3) no opinion   (4) disagree   (5) strongly disagree   (N/A) not applicable

When using Elon's Interlibrary Loan services:

It is easy to request materials through Interlibrary Loan.	1	2	3	4	5	N/A
I am notified promptly of any problems, delays, or unusual charges for these services.	1	2	3	4	5	N/A
My requests are filled accurately.	1	2	3	4	5	N/A
The items I request arrive quickly enough for my needs.	1	2	3	4	5	N/A
The library contacts me quickly, as soon as the items I requested have arrived.	1	2	3	4	5	N/A
The loan period for items borrowed is adequate for my needs.	1	2	3	4	5	N/A
The items I request should be purchased by the library.	1	2	3	4	5	N/A
I know all I need to about policies, procedures, and the status of my requests.	1	2	3	4	5	N/A
I am able to request sufficient items at one time.	1	2	3	4	5	N/A
I am able to obtain any type of material I need using these services.	1	2	3	4	5	N/A
I want to be able to send all of my requests to the library electronically.	1	2	3	4	5	N/A
The library should offer electronic delivery of articles to my workstation.	1	2	3	4	5	N/A

6.   How would you like the library to improve in obtaining materials from other sources? _____

Please return to: **Belk Library**
ILL Department
2550 Campus Box

Elon University

Today's date_____

Please assist us in surveying Sunday use of Belk Library. THANK YOU for your help!

You are:

_____Freshman	_____Elon faculty or staff
_____Sophomore	_____Community user
_____Junior	_____Student from another school
_____Senior	_____Campus visitor
_____Graduate student	

What is your primary reason for being in Belk today?
_____Computer and/or printer use
_____Studying with a group
_____Studying alone
_____Use reserve material
_____Check out or return books or DVDs
_____Consult with librarian
_____To visit Media Services
_____Other – please explain

Library services are available Sundays from noon until 1 a.m., with the first floor staying open all Sunday night for study and computer use. Are these hours generally adequate for your needs?

_____Yes   _____No

How likely are you to come to the library if it opened before noon Sunday mornings?
_____Never
_____Only at exam time
_____Once or twice a semester
_____Monthly
_____Weekly

Normal library hours are:
Monday – Thursday – 7:30 a.m. – 1:00 a.m., followed by After Hours
Friday – 7:30 a.m. – 9:00 p.m.
Saturday – 9:00 a.m. – 9:00 p.m.
Sunday – noon – 1:00 a.m., followed by After Hours all night

Do you have any comments on library hours in general?

Do you have any concerns about weekend hours of other offices located in Belk Library?

Documents: Special Services Surveys - 110

Library Instruction -- Class Feedback

Please fill out the following course evaluation for the Library Instruction session(s) provided to your class. Check the answers that best apply.

1) Your status:

- ○ Freshman
- ○ Sophomore
- ○ Junior
- ○ Senior
- ○ Graduate

2) This course is offered by the College of (check one)

- ○ Liberal and Fine Arts
- ○ Education
- ○ Business Administration
- ○ Agriculture and Human Sciences
- ○ Science and Technology

3) The library instruction session offered information relevant to my specific research needs.

- ○ Strongly agree
- ○ Agree
- ○ No opinion/does not apply
- ○ Disagree
- ○ Strongly disagree

4) As a result of the library instruction session, I understand how to begin my research.

- ○ Strongly agree
- ○ Agree
- ○ No opinion/does not apply
- ○ Disagree
- ○ Strongly disagree

5) The library instruction session helped me understand when it is best to use the

	Strongly agree	Agree	No opinion/does not apply	Disagree	Strongly disagree
Library Catalog	○	○	○	○	○
Online databases	○	○	○	○	○

Documents: Special Services Surveys - 111

	Strongly agree	Agree	No opinion/does not apply	Disagree	Strongly disagree
Internet sites	○	○	○	○	○
Print resources	○	○	○	○	○

6) As a result of the library instruction session, I understand the difference between library databases and sites freely available on the Internet.

○ Strongly agree
○ Agree
○ No opinion/does not apply
○ Disagree
○ Strongly disagree

7) As a result of the library instruction session, I understand how to create effective searches using the

	Strongly agree	Agree	No opinion/does not apply	Disagree	Strongly disagree
Library catalog	○	○	○	○	○
Online databases	○	○	○	○	○
Internet search engines	○	○	○	○	○
Print resources	○	○	○	○	○

8) The library instruction session had a positive impact on the research I did for this class.

○ Strongly agree
○ Agree
○ No opinion/does not apply
○ Disagree
○ Strongly disagree

9) Additional comments:

Thank you for your time in completing this survey. NOTE: This survey has been reviewed by the Subcommittee for University Surveys of the University Planning Council at Tarleton State University in Stephenville, Texas. If you have questions concerning this review process, please contact the Director of the Office of Planning, Evaluation, and Institutional Research at (254) 968-9354.

Reference Satisfaction Survey

PLEASE LET US KNOW HOW WE ARE DOING. Evaluate the REFERENCE service you received today by completing the survey below.

1) Your campus:

- ○ Stephenville
- ○ Killeen
- ○ Other (please specify)

If you selected other, please specify:

2) Your status:

- ○ Tarleton Undergraduate
- ○ Tarleton Graduate Student
- ○ Faculty
- ○ Research Staff
- ○ Staff
- ○ Other (CTC student, high school student, guest)

3) Your college:

- ○ Liberal and Fine Arts
- ○ Education
- ○ Business Administration
- ○ Agriculture and Human Sciences
- ○ Science and Technology
- ○ Not applicable

4) Reference service you used today:

- ○ In person, in the building
- ○ Emailed a question
- ○ Other (please specify)

If you selected other, please specify:

5) To what extent were you satisfied with:

Not satisfied	Somewhat dissatisfied	Neither satisfied nor	Satisfied	Very satisfied

			dissatisfied		
Relevance of the information	○	⊠	○	⊠	⊠
Amount of information provided	⊠	⊠	○	⊠	○
Completeness of the answer you received	○	⊠	○	⊠	○
Helpfulness of the staff	○	⊠	○	⊠	○

6) Overall, how satisfied are you with the service you received today?

○ 1 (Not satisfied)
○ 2
○ 3
○ 4
○ 5 (Very satisfied)

7) Why?

8) My reference questions were for:

○ Course work
○ Research
○ Teaching
○ Current awareness
○ A mix of several reasons
○ Other (please specify)

If you selected other, please specify:

9) Additional Comments: